Organize Your Home

by Christi Youd

www.organizeenterprise.com

P.O. Box 876 American Fork, UT 84003.
Telephone 801-756-3382.
FAX 801-763-9577.
Email: christi@OrganizeEnterprise.com
Web: www.OrganizeEnterprise.com

Table of Contents

1

Minimize the Maintenance

Some years ago, I was, shall we say, not very organized when it came to managing a clean home, having clean clothes available, or having hot meals prepared on time. On one particular day, I had dishes from the night before filling my sinks and covering the counters. There were newspapers, old food particles, and sticky who-knows-what all over the table and bar. I had piles of laundry covering my couch and love seat. I hadn't bothered showering yet and I was dressed in sweats, which were too small, a sweatshirt covered in stains, no make-up, and my hair pressed against my head on one side and sticking out every direction on the other side of my head from sleeping on it the night before.

I had this bright idea that this would be the day to put up all the Christmas decorations. That was a big job, so I didn't take time to clean up first. I jumped right into the project. I went down to the basement and pulled up seven big Rubbermaid totes full of decorations. I proceeded to spread their contents into piles all over my kitchen and living room, mixed in with the laundry, dishes, etc. What a mess! I was exhausted, so I decided to go upstairs to sit in my rocker and do some "think work" for a while.

I came downstairs a couple of hours later and there in the middle of this mess (far away from the front door) was a check from my neighbor and friend. I know the check was not there when I went upstairs. Of course, she had to be the one person in the neighborhood who was always so well organized and put together. I could just imagine how this neighbor must have cracked open the front door to set the check inside, saw what a mess there was, and felt afraid that I'd never find the check. She walked into the house a little bit to set it on the kitchen counter, where I'd be sure to see it, only to find an even bigger mess in there. Finally, giving up on the idea of finding a place I would be sure to see the check, she put it in the cleanest spot she could find and hightailed it out of the house before I caught her there. I'm sure she didn't want to have to pretend that all was well in the land of chaos.

I was standing there in all my glory, staring at that check and experiencing a state of panic, shame, urgency, and mortification. How could I ever face that neighbor again? No amount of explaining could undo the impression made on her that day. What was I going to do?

I vowed then and there I would never get caught like that again. I was determined to get organized. Organizing became my life study. Eventually, I became a Professional Organizer, and through my association with the National Association of Professional Organizers and an endless amount of personal study, I learned the proven strategies for becoming an organized home manager. I am excited to share them with you. Just know that if your life is disorganized or a bit of a mess, I understand. I pass no judgment.

Right brain vs. left brain

There is a theory out there about right – and left-brained people. If you are predominantly left-brained, organization comes pretty easily to you. It seems only natural. But, if you are predominantly right-brained, like me, it doesn't come quite so easily. Our overactive right brain is highly creative and spontaneous. It is fun-loving. It makes us great at interacting, but not so great at acting.

The Pharmacy

I'll give you an extreme example of the difference between a right brain person and a left brain person. As a teenager, I worked in the pharmacy of our small town drug store. One day I took a call and was speaking with a lady about her prescriptions. In the gift aisle (the one with all the glass ornaments and porcelain dolls) the casing of florescent lights detached from the ceiling and crashed to the floor breaking everything in its path. It made an incredible noise.

I didn't stop to assess the situation. I didn't consider the options and then make the best choice. I didn't even stop to put down the phone. I simply ran as fast as I could out the back door, with the phone still up to my ear. When I ran out of cord, the phone snapped out of my hand and hit the wall; I kept going. I knew the sky was falling and we were all going to die! That casing of lights pulled down the next casing of lights, "crash," and the next casing, "crash," until the entire aisle was annihilated.

When the dust finally settled and I decided it was safe to go back inside, I stepped over the mess and went into the pharmacy. The phone was still dangling there, so I grabbed it to hang it up. As I did so, I heard that woman on the line still talking about her prescriptions. She had not missed a beat. She had heard that incredible noise, but she had a task to perform and nothing was going to keep her from getting her task done: a typical left-brain person behavior. Whereas I, on the other hand, was completely off in a new direction at the first sign of distraction: a typical right-brain person behavior.

Let me explain why it's so hard to stay organized if you are right-brained. Because our right brain is overactive, we jump into projects with great enthusiasm and imagination. But, as soon as we hit the boring part of the project, our right brain causes thoughts to come into our head of other things we should be doing. ("Oh, I need to call so and so!" or "I'm hungry, what is there to eat?" or "Ugh! I was going to get such and such done today!") These thoughts cause us to shift our activity without completing the project we are on. The thoughts make it very difficult to stay focused and productive on any project. In other words being a right brain person really makes it difficult to work in an organized manner. Organization doesn't come naturally to right-brained people, *but it can be learned.*

What you want to do is develop the skill of disregarding those thoughts. Recognize that your brain is bored. It is going to produce all kinds of thoughts and ideas to try to get you to stop doing what you are doing because it's become boring, and switch to something more fun loving, interesting, and stimulating. Tell your right brain who is boss. Refuse to switch gears until you have completed the project you are currently working on. Just Say No! You are not going to do that idea. No! You are not going to give in to those thoughts. Recognize those thoughts and ideas as the distraction and obstacle they are to your productivity. Once you are able to recognize and deal with those right brain messages, getting organized will be a breeze.

The Decision

Another part of mind awareness is your decision-making ability. Have you made the decision to get organized yet? I'm not asking if you recognize the need to get organized, or that life would be better if you were organized. I'm asking if you have made the decision that you are getting organized. It must be a true decision! You see -*cision* means to cut and *de* – means away from. So, when you make a true decision to change a behavior, you literally cut yourself away from the previous behavior. What are your chances of truly getting organized if you have decided to stop (cut yourself away from) being disorganized? The other criterion for a true decision is that action has to be derived from it. If your decision doesn't result in action, it's just daydreaming or wishful thinking.

Do you know you should eat healthfully and exercise, but you don't actually do either on a consistent basis? Just the same, you may have *the desire* to get better organized, but until you make a true decision to do so, what you learn here is going to be like the unapplied nutritional or aerobic advice you've simply filed away in your knowledge sector. It won't really impact your life.

Excuses

When we consider why we're not already organized, we find a myriad of reasons and extenuating circumstances for why it hasn't happened. When we are feeling brave and are prepared to call a spade a spade, we recognize that those reasons and extenuating circumstances are just other words for excuses. You have a simple choice: You can hang onto your excuses, or let them go. By hanging on, you stay in the mess you are in. But if you recognize that excuses won't help you get out of your mess, you can make the true decision to stop hanging onto your excuses. Those excuses are keeping you from getting what you want. Let go of them no matter how valid, legitimate, or reasonable they may seem to be.

The Seven Steps and Seven Strategies That Keep You Organized

If someone were to put in front of you everything you are supposed to eat from now until you are 95 years old, and tell you that you had to eat all of it by yourself, it would probably feel like a daunting task. If they were to mix it all together it probably wouldn't look very appetizing either. But, because we break it down into portions that we are going to eat each day (which get broken down into meals, which get further broken down into courses in the meal) and because we only have to eat when our hunger pains drive us to do so, it becomes much more manageable. It is doable.

Patricia had the ability to walk into a room and in a matter of seconds she would take note of a dozen things that needed to be done in the room. Along with that observation, she would register that she was going to have to do those things again and again and again, making the task bigger and more daunting. Finally she would think, "I can't deal with that right now" and she would walk into the next room; only to have the exact same thing happen there. It's like looking at that huge pile of food and feeling like she needed to eat it all immediately. Most of us are like Patricia. When we think about getting our entire homes organized we are overwhelmed and can't figure out how to get the job done.

The following chapters will help you break the organizing process down into steps comparable to meal-size portions, making it manageable and doable. You do it one step at a time. But here is the best part of what is yet to come: Have you ever organized an area in your home only to have that organization fall apart and you find yourself back at square one once again? What's the joy in that? Not only will the following chapters teach you the seven basic steps that will get your home organized, but they are also going to teach you the seven key strategies that make it *stay* organized.

The reason our business is so successful is because we make a bold promise and we deliver on that promise. Our promise is that we will organize your home, office, or business so you are in a position to function at your very best, feel great about the way your space looks, and be able to maintain it in as little as 10 minutes a day. We go so far as to guarantee our work. Our guarantee states that if we organize your space, and if you follow our recommendations, your space will stay organized for at least seven years. If it does not, we will come back and organize it again at no charge.

How can we dare to make such a bold promise? We don't organize things the traditional way. I'm not saying we don't follow standard organizing principles. I'm just saying we have sought out the principles that ensure a lasting outcome, and we live strictly by those principles. We organize everything with three outcomes in mind:

- It has to be a system that will help you function

at your very best.

- It needs to be a system that will STAY organized.
- It has to be a system that will require a minimum amount of maintenance.

We want to help people break free of clutter and chaos, but we also want them to break free of hours and hours of maintenance. Organizing is fun, but there are so many other beneficial and worthwhile activities in life. You don't want to have to organize your life again and again.

How do we do it? We follow seven simple strategies, and we put them in place in everything we do.

Strategy #1: Do All Seven Steps of the Organizing Process

The Seven Steps of the organizing process are as follows:

1. Examine your situation
2. Design a plan that works for your situation
3. Categorize your things
4. Haul things to their new destination
5. Assign the right home for your things
6. Obtain the right containers
7. Sustain your systems through daily maintenance.

Take the time to carefully examine your situation and design a plan that will work with your habits, style, needs, and priorities before you sort through anything. You will make key distinctions during your examination which will alter the plans you design for how to organize. Those alterations will create an entirely different result than you would have otherwise achieved. The difference in those results makes all the difference in whether your space stays organized for a few weeks or for a lifetime.

Categorize your things. Weed out the 80% of your things you are not actually using on a regular basis. Clear out the excess clutter so you won't have to deal with it anymore. Hauling things off, assigning the right home to the items you keep, and obtaining the right containers for those items all impact how well your things will stay organized.

Sustaining your systems on a daily basis determines how well it stays organized. If we were to claim your organized systems would last without any effort on your part to maintain them, you would be justified in bringing out the straightjackets. Common sense dictates that it is going to require some type of maintenance. This maintenance must be done daily. Not weekly. Not monthly. Not quarterly. It must be done daily. If you maintain it daily, and if you have the Seven Strategies in place, you should be able to maintain your organization in just 10 minutes a day.

Strategy #2: Insist on a proper fit between your things and the container you are putting them into. Insist on a proper fit between your containers and the space you are going to keep the containers.

Peter had let his top desk drawer become his "stash drawer." The drawer was 3 inches high, 18 inches wide and 18 inches deep. Peter had tried to get his drawer organized before and had purchased a little drawer organizer that was ½ inch high, 6 inches wide, and 10 inches deep. It wasn't big enough to contain all the things he needed to keep in that drawer, so it was surrounded on all sides by the things that would not fit in the organizer. There was a 2½ inch space between the top of the organizer and the top of the drawer. It left ample space to stash papers and miscellaneous items he didn't want to deal with. Whenever he needed something out of the drawer he would; open it, pull out the pile of papers and miscellany, and scoot the organizer and things surrounding it out of his way until he could find the item he needed. Then he put the organizer back, stuffed the papers and other paraphernalia back on top of it, and shut the drawer. Many times he couldn't find what he was looking for.

The drawer organizer was not the right fit for the drawer. We got rid of the drawer organizer. We ordered drawer dividers that allow you to place items where you want them and then build walls around them so there is an exact fit. The new dividers were three inches high and eliminated the opportunity for Peter to stash things on top. They gave every item in the drawer its own reserved home.

Build a custom drawer organizer with drawer dividers.

We worked with Stephanie to organize her bathroom linen closet. It was a double wide closet with four deep shelves in it. She had purchased several plastic bins which were only half the depth of the shelves. Because she needed to use all her space, she started shoving stuff loosely behind the containers. Before she knew it, she was pulling out the containers to look behind them and not caring if it all became disorganized. We measured the shelves, purchased enough containers to consume 80% of the shelf space, and installed the containers. The shelves were deep so we put a row of containers on the back of the shelf and another row of containers on the front of the shelf. We labeled the containers and the places where the containers belonged. There was enough space between the top of the containers and the shelf above it that she could reach in and put things away with one swift motion. She could easily retrieve the items she needed without having to move the containers. Now the closet could contain everything and stay organized. The closet has gone years without having to be reorganized, and she can find whatever she needs in a fraction of the time.

Establish a proper fit on your shelves.

It's not enough to want or hope for a proper fit. You must *insist* on a proper fit. *Insist* on a proper fit between the size of the room and the size and amount of furniture and equipment you keep in that room. Most people try to cram far more furniture into a room than that room was really designed to hold. *Insist* on a proper fit between the furniture and equipment and the number and sizes of containers you keep in the furniture and equipment. *Insist* on a proper fit between the size of your containers and the number and size of things you keep in your containers. When you are doing your categorizing step and sorting out all the excess, remember that above all you must obtain a proper fit between the room, the containers, and your things.

A proper fit is about 80% of the capacity. You want to leave enough room for things and people to flow throughout the space. You want to leave room for you to grow. Believe me, in our society, the amount of stuff you accumulate will grow!

A proper fit means not too big and not too small. Containers that are too big or too small will cause things to get disorganized. Get good at taking measurements before you move furniture or buy containers.

It's going to be a bit of a challenge to find containers you like that are exactly the right size. You'll have to spend a little more time searching. Remember once you find the container it will be in your home working on your behalf for many years to come. I like to shop online because I can quickly ascertain the size of the containers and look through several stores' selections in a very short time. Take measurements. Take your time finding the right containers. While appearance is important, having the right dimensions should be a higher priority than appearance. Getting the right dimensions will help you to function at your very best, feel great about the way your space looks, and be able to maintain your space in as little as 10 minutes a day.

Strategy #3: Store items at the place they are first used.

It's human nature to take the path of least resistance. If a person finishes using an item, and putting it away where it belongs is kind of a pain but leaving it out is fairly easy, they are going to leave it out. You want to make putting items away where they belong as easy as possible. People will put things away more often if the home where the item belongs is right there where they've been using it. If they have to walk into another room to put it where it belongs, they will tend to leave it out "just for now."

Strategy #4: Make it easier to put an item away than it is to get it out.

This is the opposite of traditional organizing. It follows the premise that if it's fairly difficult to get out, but you need it, you will go to the effort to get it. However, if it is fairly difficult to put it away, you'll probably leave it out "for now." This will cause your organization to fall apart over time. But don't overdo it. You don't want to make it downright difficult to get something out. You want it to be just barely easier to put it away than it is to get it out.

Rebecca had over 300 videos. Her children and grandchildren were known to never put the videos back into their cover and onto the bookshelf where they belonged. Rebecca was highly frustrated at how frequently she had to match videos up with their covers and put them away on the shelf. She was frustrated with the pile of videos and covers that continued to sprawl out in front of her television.

Rebecca stored her videos on a bookshelf. The bookshelf was positioned on the opposite end of the room from the VCR. She felt that arrangement made the room look the most attractive. Her children and grandchildren had to walk over to the bookcase and pick out the video they wanted to watch. They would walk across the room to put it into the VCR. They would take the video out of its cover and since there was no place (right there) to put the cover they would drop it on the floor in front of the television. Then they would try to put the video into the VCR. There would already be a video in the VCR so they had to eject the old video before putting in the new video. Since there was no place (right there) to put the old video, they would put it on the floor in front of the television. Then they would push play and sit down to watch the video.

We looked at the scenario and asked ourselves, "How can we organize these videos so it is easier to put the videos away than it is to get them out?" We ended up moving the bookcase over to be right next to the VCR. This made it easy to reach while standing in front of the VCR – without traveling. Then we packed up all the covers and put them into storage. Rebecca wasn't prepared to throw away the covers until she tested the system to see how she liked it. We put a big bold label on the spine of every video and we stacked them side by side on their end so you could see all the spines.

Each bookshelf was labeled with a different category (animated, action, comedy, etc.). When the grandchildren wanted to choose a video, they had to go to the category they wanted, tip their heads to the side and read the labels to see what the movies were. They no longer had the pictured covers to help them recognize their favorite videos.

They would grab the video they wanted to watch and try to put it into the VCR. They would have to eject the old video before they could put in the new video. Since the bookshelf was right there and since they no longer had to worry about matching the videos up with their covers they were able to stick the video they ejected onto the appointed bookshelf – without traveling.

Putting the videos away now required one swift motion. It was actually easier to put the videos away than it was to get them out. Cleaning up the videos was never an issue for Rebecca again. She didn't spend any time matching videos to their covers. There were no piles of videos or covers on the floor in front of the television.

This is just one example of making it easier to put an item away than it is to get it out. Notice the videos were still organized. Leaving them in a pile in the middle of the room would be easier to put them away than it was to get them out, but that would not be organized. They still need to be highly accessible and organized in such a way they are well preserved.

Strategy #5: Eliminate extra steps in the putting away process.

After attending one of our speeches, Margaret organized her bathroom closet. She had put everything into clear containers and had them properly labeled. She was careful to not stack the containers so she wouldn't have to lift containers off in order to put things away. When she first organized the closet it looked awesome. All the containers had color-coordinated lids. All the labels were professionally made and looked really sharp. It was a closet that Better Homes and Gardens would be proud of. Three months later the containers were buried and surrounded with clutter.

As we walked through the putting away process with her looking at every motion, we saw what caused the system to break down. Whenever she had something that needed to be put in the containers she usually had her hands full with other things. Since taking the lid off, putting the items inside, and putting the lids back on required two hands and called for three motions, she avoided doing it. Instead she would just set the items on top of the container, or beside it, or in front of it, with the intent to put it inside the next time her hands were free or she had the time. We encouraged her to get rid of the lids. Putting the items inside the containers would be as easy as leaving them on the outside. Her things would stay organized in the container they were intended for. She had a hard time letting go of the lids. It seemed unnatural for her. Eventually she got rid of them, and her closet has stayed organized ever since.

If it's not absolutely necessary to keep the lid on your container, get rid of it. That will save you two motions every time you get something out or put it back.

Any time you find something being left out repeatedly, walk through the putting away process for that item. Pay attention to how many motions it takes to put it away. Do what you can to change the putting away process so it can be done in fewer motions.

Strategy #6: Label, Label, Label!!!

Labeling helps everyone in the family to know exactly where everything belongs. It trains us to put things away in the same place every time. It causes our things to stay organized even when life requires our focus somewhere else.

Strategy #7: Maintain it daily.

If you have the Seven Strategies in place throughout your home, you should be able to maintain it in just 10 minutes a day. Pick a time of day when you can call your family together and race through the house picking things up that have been put in the wrong place and putting them where they really belong.

> Ruth enters the family room and she asks son, Michael, to check the drawers and shelves in the entertainment center for things that are out of place. She asks her husband, Daniel, to check the family room game closet and cupboards for things that are out of place. She and her daughter Stephanie walk through the room and look for things on the floor and furniture that have been left out. There are very few things left out, and since the home for those items is right there in the family room, they are able to quickly and easily put them where they belong. In just a few seconds the family moves into the kitchen to make sure everything is in its place in there.

That is a brief introduction to the Seven Strategies that will keep your home organized. In the following chapters, we will take a more in depth look at the Seven Steps of the organizing process and the application of the Seven Strategies in every room and every item found in a typical home.

2

The Organizing Process

I want you to imagine yourself in a huge mess consisting of piles of bricks and bags of mortar. Now, clean up the mess and get it all organized. How would you do it? Most people would answer that question by saying they would stack the bricks and bags of mortar into neat piles.

Why didn't you build your dream home with those bricks?

When people think about getting organized, they generally think of having all their things neat and tidy. What if you were to organize, so you were creating your family's dream home rather then just tidying it up? What if you were actually able to shape each room so it supports you in the activities that are the most important to you?

It takes work

Having your home well organized, in a manner that stays well organized, is a blessed outcome. Getting yourself in the position where your home stays clutter-free and organized with just 10 minutes of maintenance each day is a goal worth striving for. But don't kid yourself – it's going to take some work on your part to get it that way, but once you get what you want, it is all worthwhile.

E.N.D. C.H.A.O.S.

Many people limit the organizing process to three steps. They:

1) sort through their things

2) decide where to put them, and

3) put them into containers.

I am going to ask you to change your thinking. I want you to understand that there are actually Seven Steps in the organizing process. I introduced you to them briefly in the previous chapter, and we'll discuss them in greater detail as we go along. Doing all Seven Steps as opposed to only three makes all the difference in how long your organization will last. In fact out of the strategies that cause your things to STAY organized, doing all Seven Steps of the organizing process is the #1 strategy. It makes the biggest difference.

It is important that you follow the Seven Steps in the right order. Each step's completion affects what you need to do in the following steps. For example, sorting through your things and getting rid of some of them alters the size container you will need. If you purchased your container before you sorted through your things, you would end up with the wrong size container. If you try to complete the steps in the wrong order, you will experience a lot of frustration and you will not be happy with the results.

It is also important that you complete each step before moving on to the next one. One thing I have noticed people doing is start sorting through their things, and before they know it they have stopped sorting and have started deciding where to put their things, and then, in the middle of that activity, they are planning what containers they need. They end up working in circles, not really making any progress. They are moving things, and making piles, but not really going anywhere or getting anything accomplished. Just like the shortest distance between two points is a straight line, disciplining yourself to work on one step at a time, and completing each step before moving on to the next will keep you on the shortest path to an organized, clutter-free home.

To help you remember the steps in order, I have created the acronym, "E.N.D. C.H.A.O.S."

*E*xamine Your Situation

a*N*d

*D*esign a Plan that Works for Your Unique Situation

*C*ategorize Your Things

*H*aul Them to Their New Destinations

*A*ssign the Right Home

*O*btain the Right Container

*S*ustain Your Systems Daily

Now, the objective is to end chaos in your home. However, most people begin to organize by diving straight into the sorting process, leaving out the steps of **e**xamine and **d**esign (E.N.D.). Without E.N.D., all you are left with is C.H.A.O.S., which is exactly what happens to the space you've organized in about four weeks' time.

Taking the time to properly examine your situation and design a plan that will work best for it will dramatically increase the chances of achieving a dream home that stays organized.

3

Examine Your Situation

The "E" in E.N.D. C.H.A.O.S. stands for Examine Your Situation. This is the first step in the organizing process. A complete examination consists of four different areas of discovery:

- Why do you want to get organized?
- What is already happening?
- What do you want to have happen?
- What is causing the disorganization in your home?

I recommend you get a new notebook for your "Organized Home" notes. Think through the following considerations and write everything down. You will refer to your notes often while designing your plan.

When you are examining your situation you want to take many things into consideration, so you don't end up with a disappointing result.

As you examine your situation, consider each of the following questions:

Why do you want to get organized?

With every achievement, 10% is to knowing *how* to do it and 90% is knowing *why* you are doing it.

Sorting through all of your stuff and getting rid of things you've been hanging onto can be painful. If you are not clear about why you are doing it, you are not going to do it. At least, you won't do it thoroughly.

Getting all the stuff in your house organized is a lot of work. You are not going to see it through, unless you have a big enough reason *why!*

To give you a realistic picture of what it would take to transform your home let me share the following statistics:

Room	Average time needed to complete all Seven Steps of the organizing process
kitchen, bedroom, living room, family room, laundry room, bathrooms, gathering room, dining room	15 hours (each)
home office, garage, storage room, unfinished basement	30 hours (each)
typical 3-bedroom home	240 hours (total)

Now, whatever you do, don't stop reading here. At least finish this chapter!

Remember, it took you a long time to get your house in the condition it is in now. Getting it organized isn't going to happen overnight; but it can, and will, get organized if you set up a schedule and stay committed. Let me give you a couple of scenarios.

> Vicky decided to complete one room per month. It was a relaxed enough pace that it didn't overwhelm her while working part time and raising two preschoolers. She kept at it, and in one year her home was made new. She enjoyed the benefits for many years to come.

> Janet couldn't stand the idea of waiting a full year to have her home done. She set the pace of one room per week. This was a much more intense schedule, but she realized the end results and benefits in a fourth of the time. Janet knew if she didn't hit it hard she would lose her focus and it would never get done. The intense pace and schedule worked for her.

Do what works for you. Set a realistic schedule and stay committed until the job is completely done. It will take some work, but words cannot express how sweet it is to have a well-organized home that only takes 10 minutes a day to maintain.

If the amount of work involved is enough to discourage you, try the following exercise. It will help you determine if the work involved in getting your home organized will be worth it.

Establish the right mindset about de-cluttering and organizing.

The information that follows is an excerpt from my *"30 Days to a Clutter-free Home Coaching Program."* For more details on the coaching program, go to www.OrganizeEnterprise.com/coaching. This segment of the coaching program was designed to help you establish the right mindset about de-cluttering and organizing.

Have you ever wanted to lose weight or get into better physical condition? You learned the right way to eat healthily and exercise. But even though you gained the knowledge of how to diet and exercise, you couldn't get yourself to actually do it on a consistent basis.

Have you ever wanted to save your money for something, but something else came along that caused you to spend your money elsewhere. Perhaps you learned how to manage your money, but in the bumpy course of life you were not able to allocate it as perfectly as you knew you should?

I've heard it said, "I know *how* to organize. I just can't bring myself to *do* it."

If you want to get your home de-cluttered and organized. It's not enough to *know how* to do it. You have to find the secret that gets you to *do* what you *know*. That secret lies in understanding how the human brain and nervous system work. Your brain and nervous system work together to keep you safe. They help you avoid pain and gain pleasure. They are always monitoring what experiences are going to lead to pain or what experiences are going to lead to pleasure. Your brain and nervous system do not drive your behavior according to the reality or the experience you have had. They drive your behavior according to their *interpretations* of the reality you experience.

There is a difference between your reality and your brains *interpretation* of that reality. Perhaps you have seen this demonstration before.

How do you interpret reality?

Some people *interpret* the picture by seeing a saxophone player. Other people *interpret* the picture by seeing a woman's face. No matter which way you interpreted it, it may take you a few minutes to <u>see</u> the other image.

The reality (which is the picture itself) didn't change. Both interpretations of the reality were there the entire time. Now, look at the picture of the de-cluttering experience you hold in your imagination. The reality may be that you significantly reduce the amount of stuff you have. One person may *interpret* that reality as a source of physical, mental, or emotional discomfort or irritation, causing feelings of loss or sacrifice, frustration, or embarrassment, a source of creating conflict with family members, or not wanting to commit to the time or energy spent on that activity.

Another person may *interpret* significantly reducing the amount of stuff they have as a source of freedom, hope, lightening their load, creating more time for them to do what they choose, making themselves and their home more comfortable physically, mentally, socially, emotionally, financially, and spiritually. They may see it as gaining more living space since less is being used for storage space, or exercising their right to shape their own environment to be the way they want it to be.

You may have the interpretation that getting your home de-cluttered requires you to sacrifice time, money, and comfort. The challenge with that interpretation is that it establishes some limitations for your life. It requires you to stay stuck in a very limited, confined reality. It's important that you remember that your interpretation is *merely an interpretation*. Study the picture in your imagination. Take a moment to find the other interpretation.

All through life you have had experiences, and your brain and your nervous system *interpreted* whether each experience was painful or pleasurable, came to conclusions about what certain things mean to you, and filed this information away. All these experiences, interpretations, and conclusions are called *neuro-associations*. When you think about de-cluttering your home, your brain researches its database looking for some reference of what that will mean to you – what you associate with it. It picks up all the little experiences, interpretations, and conclusions you have filed away. Based on what it finds, your brain will tell your nervous system that de-cluttering your home will either lead to pain or to pleasure. Your nervous system will create strong feelings throughout your system that make you either highly motivated or highly discouraged at the prospects of de-cluttering your home.

Now, in truth, what most of you develop are *mixed* associations where you associate some pain and some pleasure with de-cluttering your homes. You also associate some pain and some pleasure with leaving your homes cluttered. It creates a tug-of-war, where you want something, you begin to work on it, you sabotage your own efforts, and then you beat yourself up for sabotaging yourself. You are not 100% motivated to de-clutter your home because you link both pain and pleasure with the process.

You may be wondering what pleasure you could possibly derive from staying in a cluttered home.

When it comes to letting your cluttered home stay the way it is, you may associate:

- pleasure in the form of escaping the effort required,
- comfort in hanging onto what is familiar to you,
- joy in the activities you get to do instead of de-cluttering your home,
- satisfaction in being prepared in every occasion, or
- feelings of wealth due to the abundance of your possessions.

Here is the bottom line: If you want to be motivated to de-clutter and organize your home, you need to explore the neuro-associations your brain and nervous system have accumulated about that experience. You will then need to erase the associations you no longer want and establish new associations that will get you where you want to be. It's kind of like getting on your knees and checking out your flower garden. You examine each plant to determine if it is a flower or a weed. If it is a weed, you pull it out. You plant a beautiful flower in its place. If it is a flower, you leave it there. You may even water and fertilize it to make it stronger. If you really want a beautiful flower garden, you plant more flowers. The more flowers you plant the more beautiful your flower garden will be. In the same manner, you need to search your mind to examine your "garden" of neuro-associations. If you find you associate something negative with getting your home de-cluttered, pull it out. If you find you associate de-cluttering your home with being painful, reject those beliefs/associations and plant new ones in their place. Replace it with a positive association or affirmation. If you really want to be highly motivated, you want to plant additional associations that support your desire to have a de-cluttered home. Plant associations in your mind that if you <u>don't</u> get your house de-cluttered, it is going to lead to ultimate pain. You should plant associations that if you <u>do</u> get your house de-cluttered, it is going to lead to ultimate pleasure.

My favorite example of changing one's associations is the story of Scrooge in Charles Dickens' *Christmas Carol*. Scrooge had three "motivators" visit him in the night who helped him associate so much pain with staying the way he was that he totally changed his outlook and behavior in *one night*.

What if you were to switch the associations you have accumulated in your brain as to what will cause pain and what will cause pleasure? What if you were to discover the costs or the pain of letting your cluttered home stay the way it is? What if you were to link up so much pain to leaving it that way that you would do anything to avoid experiencing that pain? What if you were able to switch your associations of what equals pleasure? What if you saw a clutter-free home in just 10 minutes a day as something so pleasurable you would do anything to attain it? I'm going to give you some step-by-step instructions will help you do that.

Why leave the associations you have linked up in your brain to whatever has been formed by a myriad of happenstance? Why not organize your associations so they empower you to behave in accordance to what you know would make your life better? The following step by step instructions lead you in an exercise that will help you recognize the associations you currently have and teach you how to realign them. The following step-by-step instructions will help you associate pain with not de-cluttering your home and pleasure with de-cluttering your home. That way your associations will highly motivate you to *do* what you *know.*

Examining Your Neuro-Associations: Step-by-Step Instructions

Step One:

Get a notebook and pen that can be reserved for your de-cluttering project. Then find a quiet place where you will not be interrupted. Quiet your mind. You are going to write several lists on paper, then record them on an audio cassette. Listening to your audio cassette daily will keep you motivated during the entire de-cluttering process. You want to be sure to write down all your responses. Don't just think them in your head.

Today you are going to experience both pain and pleasure. The more intensely you can experience these states, the more good it will do you in changing your neuro-associations. Your nervous system has to feel the pain and pleasure at an intense enough level for it to link up new neuro-associations. Although you may feel pain in parts of the exercise, I assure you we will leave this exercise feeling pleasure. It's important that you don't leave this exercise half way through. You don't want to leave it while you are still feeling pain. Follow through to the end.

I am going to ask you to identify the many costs of having a cluttered home. These costs will be in several areas: financial, emotional, physical, spiritual, etc. This is going to require you to stretch your thinking to come up with all the ways, but it is important that you do. The more significant each one of the costs is, the more it will motivate you. Don't cut corners here. Do your very best to come up with costs in each category that are truly meaningful for you. You want to make these as heavy and as tremendous of a cost as you can. What price have you paid over the past 5-20 years? Spend some time thinking about it. Write it down. What price will you end up paying over the next 5-20 years if you continue to live in a cluttered home? These costs should be so intense for you that you can feel a physical weight bearing down on you from the heaviness of that price. Take time to feel the price you have paid and will continue to pay.

I hesitate to list possible costs for you. My experience has shown that if I suggest it, you will discount or dispute it. If you come up with it for yourself, it must be true. However, there is value in my listing some possibilities for you to consider. I strongly encourage you to give careful consideration to the possibilities I am going to list. Denial does not help you. It only keeps you stuck in the condition you have been in for some time. Break free! I believe in you. I know you can do it. Be honest and forthright about the ways clutter has cost you. Break free of clutter's bondage! You can do it.

Now that I have you too scared to begin, let's get started.

Step Two: List the ways a cluttered home has cost you *financially*.

Some financial costs you may want to consider are:

1) All the clutter in your home was purchased one way or another. You paid for it either outright or indirectly. If it was given to you, the cost of it to the person who gave it to you consumed their resources, so they were not able to financially support you in other ways. If you really want an eye-opener, walk around your home and look at the contents. Make an estimate of what those contents cost you. I want you to really come up with a dollar figure. Take time to feel the pain of that cost before moving on. Feel it as intensely as you can.

2) A highly cluttered home can be depressing. It is common for people to think "I have to get out of the house." Tell me truthfully. Have *you* ever felt like you needed to get out of the house? Did you run some errands which included some form of *shopping* where you ended up buying more stuff? Using shopping as a way to change your state of mind is a common practice. How much money have you spent over the past 20 years doing this? Be honest. Come up with a dollar figure. Take time to feel the pain before moving on. Feel it as intensely as you can.

3) What other forms of stress management have you paid for because your cluttered home was depressing or stressful? Think of all the recreational outlets you have spent money on. Going out for a dinner and a movie. Paying a babysitter. Going on vacation. Renting a video, book, or game. Purchasing fast food because you didn't have time, energy, or desire to prepare your own meals. Purchasing convenience foods at the

grocery store which are much more expensive than foods that take time to prepare. Spending time and money on hobbies and their supplies. Purchasing items to make the home more comfortable such as decorations, electronics, containers, etc. The list goes on and on. Think of these things one at a time and calculate how much you have spent over the past 5-20 years. Take time to feel the pain of those costs before moving on. Feel it as intensely as you can.

4) A cluttered home creates stress. If it is cluttered for very long, it creates a *chronic* level of stress in your system. Chronic stress contributes to a vast number of physical and mental ailments. How much money have you spent in the past 20 years on medical bills for ailments that could have been related to stress? Include doctor's visits, prescriptions, and tests, lost work, physical therapy, massages, chiropractic, psychiatric therapy, marriage counseling, hospitalizations, anesthesia, dietician, and ibuprofen. Include it all. Come up with a dollar figure of what it has cost you over the past 5-20 years. What will it cost you in the next 5-20 years if you remain in a cluttered home?

5) It is not enough that you paid for the clutter when you first acquired it. Now you are paying for it *again* by paying for the expenses of storing it and caring for it. Consider the amount you have paid in the past 5-20 years for your home mortgage, property taxes, heating and air conditioning, lighting, and the cleaning of your home. You may think, "We would have paid that anyway so we could live in the home," but if your stuff is there you are not paying for it as living space you are paying for it as storage space. Storage space for all your clutter. Take time to feel the pain before moving on. Feel it as intensely as you can.

6) Consider the lost income opportunities since your time, thoughts, and energy were consumed with managing the clutter. If you had exchanged the time spent looking for things and picking up the clutter for time spent generating income, how much could you have made over the past 5-20 years? Take time to feel the pain before moving on. Feel it as intensely as you can.

7) Consider the money you have spent hiring services from other people or companies because you didn't have time to get around to it. Home improvements, repair and maintenance, cleaning (carpets cleaned, windows cleaned, housekeeping), auto repair, auto cleaning, yard improvements, yard care, laundry or dry cleaning, Having your nails done, hair done, weight loss, clothes mended, and so forth. There are more services available than we can shake a stick at. How many services have you hired-out because you didn't have the extra resources to do it yourself? Those resources could be your time, energy, thought, effort, training, practice, or patience. If your own resources are consumed with dealing with a cluttered home you have to pay someone else for the resources to provide these services. Take time to feel the pain before moving on. Feel it as intensely as you can.

8) I had a client who lost $75,000 in one year due to late fees, penalties, and inaccurate charges. She could never find her bills to monitor them. What are you losing? Take time to feel the pain before moving on. Feel it as intensely as you can.

9) Stretch your thinking. Add to this list. Think of as many financial costs as you can. The more costs you think of the more motivated you will be to tackle this de-cluttering project.

Step Three: List the ways a cluttered home has cost you *mentally*.

Follow the same process as you did with your financial costs. Feel the pain!

Some mental costs you may want to think about are:

1) Consider your ability to concentrate. Distractions are the number one obstacle to being able to concentrate, and clutter is the number one source of distraction. It may be clutter in your home, clutter in your mind, or clutter in your schedule. Clutter-free homes allow the people living in them to laser their focus and to accomplish amazing things.

2) Consider the costs to your memory. What are the important details in life you are dedicating your memory cells to? Have your memory banks reached their full capacity remembering all the items you have? Where you saw them last? Whether or not they are in working order? Times you needed the items and couldn't find them? Also, what you could do if you can't find the items? There is not any room left in your memory for other, more important aspects of life. What ways have you spent your resources trying to help you remember things. Calendars, planners, post it notes, asking for reminder phone calls, telling your family, "Don't let me forget to..." Getting rid of the clutter-frees up so much memory space. It is unbelievable. Take time to feel the pain before moving on. Feel it as intensely as you can.

3) Consider the costs to your creativity. The *creator* of us all took chaos and *created* order. What masterpiece, whether it is writing, painting, coordinating, or whatever, is more amazing than the creative masterpiece of this earth? Take time to feel the pain before moving on. Feel it as intensely as you can.

Stretch your thinking. Add to this list. Think of as many mental costs as you can. The more costs you think of the more motivated you will be to tackle this de-cluttering project.

Step Four: List ways a cluttered home has cost you *socially*.

Follow the same process you used with your financial and mental costs. Feel the pain!

Some social costs you may want to think about are:

1) Consider the costs in your relationship with your children. What price have you paid by having your relationship with your children be one of you nagging, reminding, and complaining about the messes they left behind or how they don't help enough around the house. Imagine what kind of a relationship you could have had if you talked to them about their lives rather than about the messes they need to clean up. A clutter-free home that can be maintained in just 10 minutes a day allows you to do that. What kind of an example are you providing for your children if you live in a cluttered home? What kind of patterns are they going to follow? Are you O.K, with that? Take time to feel the pain before moving on. Feel it as intensely as you can.

2) Consider the costs in your relationship with your spouse or significant other. How happy are they to come home and be with you if the house is a mess, you are in a bad mood, the kids are unhappy and the bills are overdue? How long will they live like that before they start to look somewhere else for happiness? It's the saddest thing, but I see it happen all the time. It makes my heart sick. That is too high a price to pay! Are you going to end up paying it? Take

time to feel the pain before moving on. Feel it as intensely as you can.

3) Consider the costs in your relationship with extended family and outside community. What kind of a reputation are you establishing? How long will that reputation haunt you? I know it's tempting to hide behind our clutter so we don't have to spend any more time with extended family or community than absolutely necessary. How empty is life when the only relationships you have are with yourself and your immediate household? It might sound good for a while but in the end it is a lonely existence. Take time to feel the pain before moving on. Feel it as intensely as you can.

4) Consider the costs in your relationship with yourself. Do you experience harmony within yourself if the environment for which you have stewardship is in disarray? Isn't there some element of feeling like things are not as they should be or as you want them to be? Are you at discord with your inner self because of the condition of your home? Do you ever get to feel complete harmony and peace? How much does your cluttered home impact that? How great a sacrifice in self love, acceptance, peace, and happiness have you made? Are you really prepared to spend the rest of your life feeling that way about yourself? That is an awfully high price to pay. Take time to feel the pain before moving on. Feel it as intensely as you can.

Stretch your thinking. Add to this list. Think of as many social costs as you can. The more costs you think of the more motivated you will be to tackle this de-cluttering project.

Step Five: List ways a cluttered home has cost you *emotionally.*

Take the ways that you have been paying an emotional price all these years and let them register in your nervous system for a while. Feel the pain. Let your painful emotions allow your brain to link up so it will do anything to avoid that pain. Your brain and your nervous system will associate so much pain to a cluttered home that it will drive you to de-clutter.

Some emotional costs you may want to think about are:

1) Consider how short life is. Do you really want to spend your life filled with the emotions of shame, embarrassment, humiliation, mortification, frustration, irritation, hopelessness, exhaustion, rejection, anger, despondency, overwhelm, fear, worry, hate, dread, despair, and so on and so forth? These are the feelings experienced by people who live in homes with a lot of clutter. Maybe you think yours isn't that bad. Or maybe those feelings are so constant and familiar you don't even realize you are experiencing them. Take time to feel the pain before moving on. Feel it as intensely as you can.

2) Consider the reverse. In having a cluttered home you often sacrifice the experience of feeling comfortable, having self-respect, gratification, reassurance, happiness, feeling content with life, having hope, love, peace, harmony, satisfaction, excitement, feeling capable, having faith, belief, trust, security, anticipation, intrigue, and so on and so forth. Feel the weight of sacrificing those emotions for the past 5-20 years. COMBINED! Are you really prepared to sacrifice those emotional states for the next 5-20 years? Claim those happy states. They are yours for

the taking. De-clutter. Take time to feel the pain before moving on. Feel it as intensely as you can.

Stretch your thinking. Add to this list. Think of as many emotional costs as you can. The more costs you think of the more motivated you will be to tackle this de-cluttering project.

Step Six: List ways a cluttered home has cost you *spiritually*.

Follow the same process you have used with the other costs. Feel the burden of that weight. Feel the pain!

1) Consider the cost in your relationship with your creator. Is your creator proud of you for the condition in which you live? Do you feel close to your creator when you are filled with all the negative emotions listed above? Consider the spiritual growth you have sacrificed because you have spent your time looking for things you need and cleaning up clutter. Instead you could have spent your time studying, practicing, and perfecting spiritual aspects of your life. What are the immediate consequences of those sacrifices? What are the long term consequences of those sacrifices? How many of your loved ones do those consequences impact? Are you willing to live with those consequences? What is the price in spiritual development you have been paying for the past 5-20 years? What are you committed to doing from here on out?

Take time to feel the pain before moving on. Feel it as intensely as you can.

2) Consider your spirit. Is who you are as a spirit much more than you have been demonstrating here on earth? Have you been sacrificing the opportunity to once and for all make your life here on earth consistent with the quality of your spirit which is who you really

are? Are you willing to continue making that sacrifice for the rest of your life? What will that mean for you? It's just my opinion, but I think that would be ultimate pain. To stay so distracted by our cluttered disorganized lives that we never manifest our full potential. It's time to shout from the rooftops, "I will not be denied! And so I must de-clutter!" Take time to feel the pain before moving on. Feel it as intensely as you can.

Stretch your thinking. Add to this list. Think of as many spiritual costs as you can. The more costs you think of the more motivated you will be to tackle this de-cluttering project.

Step Seven: List ways a cluttered home has cost you *physically.*

Follow the same process you have used with the other costs. Feel the pain!

Some physical costs you may want to consider are:

1) When I ask people how a cluttered home affects them physically, the most common response I get is it makes them tired. Often it is not the work we have done that makes us feel tired it is the amount of work we recognize we still need to do. How much time have you spent feeling tired? What did that feeling of fatigue cost you in your productivity?

Take time to feel the pain before moving on. Feel it as intensely as you can.

2) Clutter affects the sanitation conditions of the home. Poor sanitation has a negative affect on your physical well being. How many germs have multiplied in your residence because of the happy habitat made available with your stacks of clutter? How many of those germs have you touched, breathed, or spread over the past

5-20 years. How much time have you spent feeling sick instead of healthy? Take time to really think about it. Take time to feel the pain before moving on. Feel it as intensely as you can.

3) I mentioned earlier how chronic clutter creates chronic stress in your system. Chronic stress causes a great number of physical and emotional health problems. What are the health problems you have had over the past 5-20 years? How many of those could have possibly been stress related? Take time to feel the pain before moving on. Feel it as intensely as you can.

4) Consider the costs you have paid in your physical fitness. You have wasted a lot of time looking for things you need or picking up the clutter. You could have spent that time on an exercise routine or on preparing food that would keep you fit. If you had, how would your physique look today? How many pounds of fat have you been carrying around day after day because of that sacrifice you have made? How much energy have you missed out on because of the proportion of your body mass that is simply fat? What could you have enjoyed with those energy reserves? Take time to feel the pain before moving on. Feel it as intensely as you can.

5) Consider the costs in your physical grooming. What if you spent the time, money, and energy on developing a fantastic wardrobe, doing your nails, hair, teeth, skin, etc? What costs have you paid because you didn't look as nice as you could have? How much time have you spent not feeling good about yourself because of the way you look? Take time to feel the pain before moving on. Feel it as intensely as you can.

Stretch your thinking. Add to this list. Think of as many physical costs as you can. The more costs you think of the more motivated you will be to tackle this de-cluttering project.

Step Eight: List 20 *negative* things you associate with a clutter-free home.

These could include:

- What you think about people who keep a clutter-free home.

- What you think it means if you always have a clutter-free home.

- What it is going to take to maintain a clutter-free home.

- Why you don't want to worry about keeping a clutter-free home.

List twenty *negative* things!

Step Nine: Write a rejection statement for each of the 20 negative things you associate with a clutter-free home.

These are statements that reject the old association. For example, they may begin with the phrase: "It is not true that..." or "I no longer believe that..." Replace your negative associations with a clutter-free home with positive affirmations that support a clutter-free home mindset using statements that begin with "I now know that..." or "I now believe..."

Step Ten: Get up and shake it off!

Get up out of your chair and stretch, bend, twist. Think happy thoughts. Plant 10 happy thoughts into your mind to interrupt the pattern of those painful thoughts. No less than 10. Do jumping jacks. Sing a happy song. Do whatever it takes to shake off the negative feelings or state you were in from doing this exercise. Then *immediately* do the following 10 steps.

Step Eleven: List ways having a clutter-free home in just 10 minutes a day will reward you *financially.*

Make these rewards as grand as possible; the bigger the better. Again, it may be a stretch for you to come up with several ways but you can do it. You must do it. You need to recognize a substantial enough reward to compel your behavior to get the job done. What are the possibilities? What financial rewards will you experience over the next 5-20 years *combined?* Take time to feel the feelings of excitement, joy, anticipation, and satisfaction upon receiving those financial rewards. These rewards should be so intense for you that you can't stay seated in your chair because they are so exciting! Get into those feelings. Take time to let the feelings of exhilaration register in your nervous system for a while. Let this help your brain link up massive amounts of pleasure with maintaining a clutter-free home. Really experience those feelings!

Some financial rewards you may want to consider are:

1) How much money will you save if you quit purchasing things that just end up being clutter? Look at the total financial costs. Multiply it by two. What would you like to do with that money? Invest it? Care for the homeless? Remodel your home or build a beautiful new home? Travel? Get a nose job? What? Imagine your checking or savings account with that much money sitting in it, waiting for you to decide what you want to do with it. Take a few minutes to daydream of what you would do with all that money. Feel the excitement, intrigue, anticipation, hope, satisfaction, joy and all the other positive states of mind you get from having that kind of money in savings. Take time to feel the pleasure of those states before moving on. Feel it as intensely as you can.

2) Consider how much more square footage you would have in your home if you didn't have any of that clutter. Would it double the amount of space you have available to set up regions (activity centers) in your home that support you in what is most important to you? Would it triple it? What regions would you set up? How much pleasure, reward, joy etc. would you experience from having those regions set up in your home? Take a few minutes to daydream about what activities you would set up in your home if you had the space. Imagine the pleasure you and your family would experience participating in those activities. Take time to feel the pleasure of those states before moving on. Feel it as intensely as you can.

3) Consider the income-generating activity you would do if you had an extra two hours a day to do it. Time you have saved by not having to look for things or picking up clutter. If you could earn that income doing something you feel passionate about or something you love doing, what would you do to earn that income? You don't have to figure out the details. Just figure out your passions and imagine spending that time doing it. Imagine you have found some way to create a fantastic income with that time. What would you do with that income? Would you put in a swimming pool? Furnish your home from top to bottom? Finance a new hobby? Further your child's education? Get completely out of debt? Double your income by investing wisely? What can you really get excited about? Take time to feel the pleasure of those states before moving on. Feel it as intensely as you can.

Stretch your thinking. Add to this list. Think of as many financial rewards as you can. The more rewards you think of the more motivated you will be to tackle this de-cluttering project.

Step Twelve: List ways a clutter-free home in just 10 minutes a day will reward you *mentally*.

Follow the same process you used for listing your financial rewards. Feel the exhilarating lift in your spirits as you think about those mental rewards.

Some mental rewards you may want to consider are:

1) Consider the possibility of boosting your ability to concentrate by 75%. What mental tasks could you accomplish with that kind of concentration? You could quickly and easily get through the tasks of daily living. Then what? Would you further your formal education? Discover the cure for cancer? Solve dilemmas in such little time you didn't even realize you were facing a dilemma? Would you design something? What would it be? Would you increase your knowledge on something that interests you? Or would you pursue the wisdom of the ages? Perhaps you would simply enjoy the freedom that comes from having things handled. Being completely free of worry or effort. Take time to feel the pleasure of the states you would experience doing those things before moving on. Feel it as intensely as you can.

2) Consider what you would retain in your memory if your memory cells were not committed to dealing with clutter. Would you memorize important writings? Would you strengthen your relationships by remembering birthdays, anniversaries, important events, or sensitive issues? What could you learn tomorrow because you still remember everything you learned yesterday? What would you gain from that? How would it benefit you? Would you like to be praised for having the memory of a steel trap where nothing escapes it? How much fun could you have with that? Take time to feel the pleasure of the states you would

experience doing those things before moving on. Feel it as intensely as you can.

Stretch your thinking. Add to this list. Think of as many mental rewards as you can. The more rewards you think of the more motivated you will be to tackle this de-cluttering project.

Step Thirteen: List ways having a clutter-free home in just 10 minutes a day will reward you *socially.*

Follow the same process you used to list your financial and mental rewards. Feel the exhilarating lift in your spirits as you think about those social rewards.

Some social rewards you may want to consider are:

1) Consider the benefits that would come from you having a better relationship with each of your children. Would you be able to influence their lives better? Perhaps help them avoid drugs, crime, unemployment, illiteracy or apathy? Perhaps you could inspire them to accomplish great things, experience great things and maintain quality relationships with others. Would you laugh with them? Feel more feelings of love and appreciation? Share an interest? If you could choose any kind of relationship to have with your children what would it be? Does it seem unreal? It doesn't have to. Take time to feel the pleasure of those states you would experience before moving on. Feel it as intensely as you can.

2) Consider the quality of relationship you would have with your spouse or significant other. Would the two of you associate feelings of happiness, enjoyment, love, passion, fascination with each other if you weren't buried by the clutter of life? Can you imagine both of you coming home and being so excited about life. Would you be full of excitement for the opportunity to

share life with each other if you weren't worried about home management responsibilities, finances, things that taxed you mentally or socially? If being free of clutter-freed you both up financially, mentally, socially, emotionally, spiritually and physically what romantic, fun, exciting, amazing thing would you share or do together? How would that improve your relationship? Would you be more attractive because you had time to take better care of yourself? Would your spouse? Take time to feel the pleasure of those states you would experience before moving on. Feel it as intensely as you can.

3) Consider the quality of relationships you will develop outside of your immediate family. What doors of opportunity will those relationships open for you? Think. Think hard.

Stretch your thinking. Add to this list. Think of as many social rewards as you can. The more rewards you think of the more motivated you will be to tackle this de-cluttering project.

Step Fourteen: List ways having a clutter-free home in just 10 minutes a day will reward you *emotionally.*

Follow the same process you used to list the other rewards. Feel the exhilarating lift in your spirits as you think about those emotional rewards. Consider the wide range of emotions you will experience when you are truly free of the clutter. Let those feelings fill your soul. Feel the joy. Feel the relief. Feel the hope. Really let your nervous system feel it.

Some emotional rewards you may want to consider are:

1) In having a clutter-free home you often enjoy feeling comfortable, having self-respect, gratification,

reassurance, happiness, feeling content with life, having hope, love, peace, harmony, satisfaction, excitement, feeling capable, having faith, belief, trust, security, anticipation, intrigue, and so on and so forth.

2) How much better will your decisions be if you are in these states when you make them? How much grander will your accomplishments be if you are always in these positive states. How much happier will you be? Really think about what it would be like to go through your life in the states I have mentioned.

Stretch your thinking. Add to this list. Think of as many rewards as you can. The more rewards you think of the more motivated you will be to tackle this de-cluttering project.

Step Fifteen: List ways having a clutter-free home in just 10 minutes a day will reward you *spiritually.*

Follow the same process you used to list the other rewards. Feel the exhilarating lift in your spirits as you think about those spiritual rewards. What will those spiritual rewards mean for you?

Some spiritual rewards you may want to consider are:

1) Consider your potential if you truly lived up to your spiritual identity.

2) Consider your strength, increased capacity, ability, happiness, and purpose.

Stretch your thinking. Add to this list. Think of as many spiritual rewards as you can. The more rewards you think of the more motivated you will be to tackle this de-cluttering project.

Step Sixteen: List ways having a clutter-free home in just 10 minutes a day will reward you *physically*.

Follow the same process you used to list the other rewards. Feel the exhilarating lift in your spirits as you think about those physical rewards.

Some physical rewards you may want to consider are:

1) What would your physique look like if you had ample time to take care of it? Would you be fit? Would you be strong? Would you be full of energy? Would you turn heads as you walked by? Consider the possibilities. Imagine the physique of your dreams and feel assured that you will have the resources to create that now that you are no longer wasting time cleaning up clutter.

2) Consider what your health would be like. You would be living in a cleaner environment. Your new zest for life would improve the quality of your health. You would have more time to eat right. Imagine having a source of energy and stamina coming from your core that helped you achieve your wildest dreams. What would it be like to FEEL healthy all the time?

3) Consider your personal grooming. Would you be well dressed? Would your teeth be straight and white if you had the funds to dedicate to that? Would your hair be groomed just the way you would like it to be because you could focus on acquiring that now? Would your nails be manicured and toes have a pedicure? Would your skin be clear because you spent the time and money getting it that way. All of these things are possible when you re-direct your time, thoughts, energy and money away from dealing with clutter towards achieving these things. How would that feel? Feel the feelings that would cause you to feel.

Stretch your thinking. Add to this list. Think of as many rewards as you can. The more rewards you think of the more motivated you will be to tackle this de-cluttering project.

Step Seventeen:

Now it's time we address your mixed emotions. We need to find the ways a cluttered home has been serving you somehow. List 20 *positive* things you associate with a cluttered home. It may be what a cluttered home says about the family. It may be what a cluttered home means about you. It may be what other benefits a cluttered home gives you. It may be about how you don't have to worry about certain things. List twenty things!

Step Eighteen: Write rejection statements for the 20 positive things you associate with a cluttered home.

These are statements that start out "It is not true that...," "I no longer believe that..." or "I now know that..." Replace your positive associations with a cluttered home with affirmations that support a clutter-free mindset.

Step Nineteen: Create a mental conditioning audio cassette.

Take the lists you have written and use them to record your costs and rewards in all the areas of your life that would be impacted by having a clutter-free home. Record the thoughts and feelings you have listed with this exercise. Describe the clutter-free home you aspire to. Describe your time freedom. What are you going to do with that time freedom? Are you going to live your passions? Pursue your dreams? Develop a talent? Relax in any way that feels good? Having a clutter-free home in just 10 minutes a day gives you two extra hours a day. You can do anything you want to do with that time. What are you going to do with it? Choose something that really lights a fire under you. Something that really gets you motivated.

Step Twenty: Listen to your audio cassette daily.

Listen to your cassette in your car, while you are getting ready for the day, while you exercise, or right when you get out of bed in the morning. You don't have to pay conscious attention to it. Just stay within earshot of it the entire time it is playing. By doing this daily mental conditioning you will boost your motivation level and move in a positive direction.

Taking it to the Next Level

In the previous exercise, you listed costs and benefits on an *intellectual* level. What you want to do now is take it to the next level where you actually *feel* the pain and pleasure. Make it an *emotional* exercise as well.

You want to create a mountain of *pain* that is so unpleasant that you will do anything to avoid it. This will move your behavior onto a path that keeps you and your home more organized. At the same time, you want to create a mountain of *pleasure* that is so enjoyable that you will do anything to obtain it. By doing this, you will be highly motivated to do the work, make the decisions, and make the time and financial investment required to get your home highly organized.

Without doing this exercise, you'll merely file this information away just like the obese population keeps a reference file on diet and exercise tips that they never implement. It won't really impact your life. It won't really move you to a better quality of life. It will just be information.

Write down the reasons why you want to get organized. Think about these reasons so intensely that you FEEL the pain and pleasure. Post the list in the room you are organizing and review it on a regular basis. This will help you do a complete and thorough job.

After you get clear on why you want to get organized, you want to spend some time clarifying what has been happening up to this point.

What is your family's organizing style?

We all know that people have their own learning style – they may learn best visually, auditorally, or kinesthetically. It doesn't mean they can't learn something using the other modalities, it just means that one modality is their dominant style of learning and it's easier for them if they have that modality involved.

What isn't as commonly known is that each family has their own organizing style, a way of keeping things organized that comes more easily to them. It doesn't mean that all the other principles of organizing don't apply, it just means they are stronger using one style than they are using the others.

If you can determine your family's organizing style and implement that style throughout the home, you will be able to set up your systems to be the *easiest and most natural* way for your family to stay organized. It will be similar to swimming with the current instead of fighting to swim upstream. You'll be amazed at how much easier it is to keep things organized.

To determine your family's organizing style, look through your home with the eyes of a stranger. In other words, without considering the history or the truth behind the matter, look at what *appears* to be fairly well organized. It's helpful to get a friend or relative to come and do this for you. They haven't been looking at your stuff day-in and day-out, and don't disqualify anything because of the story behind it. If you are going to do it yourself, use your eyes (and *only* your eyes) to see what *appears* to be relatively well-organized.

After you determine a number of places that appear to be relatively well-organized, take a good look at each of them and ask yourself: What are the logical reasons why this area has stayed organized? Some possible answers might be:

- it's a habit
- the container is a good fit for the items that go there
- it is well lit so it's comfortable to work there
- it is in a convenient location
- it is as easy to put away as it is to leave out
- it has a clearly defined and obvious home
- you straighten it every day
- everybody knows where it belongs etc.

Write down a list of reasons for each location.

Let's say you have found 12 organized locations and have written a list of four or five reasons for each location. Next compare those lists. Do any of these locations have logical reasons in common? Did convenience of location apply to more than one place? Was the location being well-lit a common reason? Find the reasons that have the highest frequency and that will reveal your family's organizing style. Once you know what seems to work for your family, you will want to implement that style throughout the house, as much as you can.

For example, in our home "Convenient Location," "Well Lit," and "Everyone Knows Where It Belongs" were the three most common reasons that defined our family's organizing style. So we simply went through the whole house and put everything in the most convenient possible location, set up extra lighting everywhere, and labeled where everything belonged. That way we were working "with the current" (our own style) rather than "swimming upstream" (expecting everyone in the family to do something they had never done before). It made maintaining a clutter-free, well-organized home much easier. That is what I'm encouraging you to do for your family: Discover your family's organizing style, and implement it throughout your home.

What are your family's habits and tendencies?

A big mistake people make when organizing their stuff is organizing it a certain way and then saying "From now on we are going to ..." They set up their organization to only stay intact if the entire family develops a new habit. Developing a new habit is good, but it can be difficult. What are the chances of every member of the family developing the same new habit at the same time? Pretty slim. So, why set up your organization so it only works if everyone in the family develops a new habit? Why set yourself up to have your organization fall apart in a very short time?

It's a great idea to constantly be working on developing better habits. But develop the habit first. Then organize to work with your habit. Don't do it the other way around.

What you want to do is look at the habits your family already has, and then set up your organization to work with those habits. For example, if the kids tend to walk in the front door and drop their coats and backpacks on the floor as soon as they walk in, put the hooks for their coats and backpacks right by the front door. If Dad and the kids tend to read in a particular chair, don't get after them to clean up the piles of books, magazines, and papers; put the bookcase close enough to that chair that they can set the reading material on the bookshelf as easily as they could let it drop to the floor. Work with your family's habits, don't fight against them.

So how do you know what your family's habits and tendencies are? Look for the piles and messes around the house. The piles tattle-tell on the behaviors. Ask yourself, "What happened there to make that mess? What habits contributed to it?" It's important to not start getting annoyed or irritated at your family's habits. Getting annoyed or irritated will cloud your heart and mind and you won't be able to creatively come up with solutions. We all have bad habits. It's part of life. Just get clear on what the habits are. Don't get judgmental or moody about it.

As I said, one way to determine your family's habits is to look at the piles throughout the house. After you look at enough piles, you will begin to recognize some of the underlying habits that contributed to them — habits that weren't obvious after just looking at one pile, but which became evident after you looked at several piles.

Another way to determine your family's habits is to spend a few minutes in each room role-playing the activities that take place in that room. Note the little things that tend to happen. Then, when you design your plan you can ask yourself, "How can I organize to work with that?" You can include solutions to work with those habits in your design.

What is not working?

Next you want to ask yourself, "What are the spaces and possessions that need to be better organized? What is simply not working the way it is?" List everything that frustrates you. You want to address all of the issues. When you organize most of a room, but leave a few things unorganized, they spill over onto the things you did organize and cause your organization to unravel. So, you want to make this list as detailed and complete as you can. Look closely at your things to stimulate your thinking. Just in case you get discouraged when looking at all the things that are not working, let me share with you an experience I had when things were not working. It will put things into proper perspective.

During Step Two of the organizing process, you will make plans for how to organize each and every one of these things that need to be better organized. It feels so awesome to have all of them addressed. It's like having a massive To Do list and getting it all checked off at once. You're free!

What are you actually using?

Make a list of what items you are actually using in your current life. Doing this before you start the sorting process will help you make better decisions on what to keep and what to get rid of.

Do this exercise. Go into any given room in the house. Look through your items and with each individual item ask yourself, "Are we actually using this on a regular basis?" Write down the long list of things you have in just that one room that you are not using on a regular basis. It's amazing how the typical American home has its rooms full of stuff, but only about 20% of it actually gets used. We'll talk more about that later in the book.

How many books do you have that you have already read? How many videos do you have that you have already watched? How many toys or games do you have that the kids don't really play with anymore? How many hobby-related items are filling your home that you don't really participate in anymore? The number of scenarios is endless.

I don't expect you to go through the entire house writing up these two lists. But do it in at least two or three rooms. It will really help you realize how much stuff you maintain that your family doesn't really use. This exercise will help you be picky about what items you will allow to stay in your home.

Getting your home organized in a manner that will stay organized requires you to take a little more space for each thing in your home. To have a home that makes it easy to maintain and keep organized, you need to clear out all the things that you don't use on a regular basis so you have enough space available for all the things you do use.

What do you want?

Get clear on what you want for yourself, your family, and your home, so that when you go to the bother of organizing your home, you will end up with each room being an environment that supports you in obtaining your most important outcomes.

What are your priorities?

I like to have my clients do the rocking chair test. Imagine yourself 95 years old, sitting in a rocker on the front porch and watching the sunset. You're reflecting on your life here on earth, recognizing it's almost over and you're asking yourself, "Did I accomplish the things I most needed to accomplish? Did I have the experiences I most wanted to have?"

What would those accomplishments and experiences be? What items in your home will help you obtain those accomplishments and experiences? You will want to have them highly accessible. What items will help you achieve and experience what you want?

Have a family discussion where everyone in the family does the rocking chair test. Find out what accomplishments and experiences are the most important to them.

What is causing your disorganization?

Anyone can tidy up a drawer. But, if you don't address what caused it to be disorganized in the first place, it's just going to get messed up again.

Some possible causes for your disorganization may include:

- A home has not been designated for every "thing."
- The homes you have designated are kind of a pain to work with or to get to.
- You have more stuff than you have space for.
- You leave things out as a reminder of what you need to do.
- You have psychological needs that cause you to be disorganized.

Let's take a closer look at each of these causes. For all examination purposes, just note which causes are a factor in your situation. You can decide what to do about them during the design step.

A home has not been designated for every "thing"

Things can't be put away if there's not a specific place where they belong. The place an item belongs is called its "home." Simply evaluate the items you have for which you have not yet designated a specific home, and designate a home for them.

Homes are a pain to work with or get to.

Either it's at an inconvenient location or access to it is hampered in some way. If putting things away is kind of a pain, you won't do it. You'll just set it some place "for now." We'll discuss some ideas on how to make your homes easy to work with a little bit later.

You have more stuff than you have space for.

If your garage, storage rooms, closets, drawers, and cupboards are full, you'll have all your surfaces covered with stuff with no way to keep it organized. There are three ways to fix this:

1) Eliminate stuff

2) Expand your storage capacity, or

3) Make the best use of every inch of storage space.

You will probably do a combination of all three. For now just decide if this cause is an issue for you.

You leave items out as a visual reminder of what you need to do.

My recommendation is to designate a closet or cupboard where you put all of your "need to do" items. Write the tasks down on a list. Let your list be your visual reminder, and keep your environment in an organized state.

Having a closet or cupboard that is only so big also helps you keep a reality check on how many projects you can actually get to. This way you may just get rid of some projects, making your to-do list more realistic.

Psychological needs that make you stay disorganized.

If you want to get organized, but you see some subtle benefits to being disorganized, you'll sabotage your efforts.

Let's address some of the most common obstacles to getting your home thoroughly de-cluttered. See the suggestions below for how you can overcome them.

De-cluttering Obstacle #1:
Keeping objects from the past.

Some people keep items, not because they are actually using them, but because they represent something from their past.

I'm not suggesting that the past is not important – of course it is. I'm a world, nation, religion, and family history buff. I derive great strength from the lives and examples of my ancestors and prominent figures and events throughout history. I think the past is extremely important. I just advocate that it is a mistake to try to keep *objects* from the past.

There are several factors that could cause you to hold onto objects from your past. Perhaps you have had loved ones who have passed away and you acquired some of their things. Perhaps you, a significant other, or a child used, wore, or did something in the past. You are keeping the object for nostalgia or keepsake purposes. Perhaps you have acquired a collection of photos, memorabilia, correspondence or other such items. Perhaps you have "stuff" that comes from past careers, hobbies, physiques, or stages of life.

I think everyone practices some form of hanging onto items that represent the past. I want us to spend a few minutes figuring out why you do that. Once you understand why you do that, and how those objects meet a need for you, you can make a conscientious choice. You can choose whether or not you want to continue to have non-living objects meet that need. You can choose to find an alternate method to meet those needs. Perhaps you'll discover a method that doesn't cause you so many problems.

I'm a big believer in need awareness and need fulfillment. I recognize that people keep "stuff" because if fulfills a need for them. I have no interest in stripping people of their needs. I have needs. I don't want anyone to expect me to give them up. What I hope to accomplish is to help you recognize what your needs are and then find a better way to meet your needs. Thus, you get to keep your needs, and you get to have your needs fulfilled. You just discover a better way to do it.

People keep objects from the past because they want the past life to continue somehow. Perhaps you feel loss if the objects from the past do not stay a part of your life. Let's dig a little deeper to see why it is so important for the objects from the past to remain a part of your life.

One reason may be because you feel like you have unfinished business which you long for the opportunity to bring closure to. Either never having said "I love you" as much as you wanted to or never getting the experiences you hoped for or wished for. Even the fact that you no longer get to experience that particular stage of life, either by yourself or with others makes you feel pain. It makes you feel like you've been cheated, as if something has been left undone. You keep hoping for closure. Even if your children are alive and still sharing life with you, they are no longer in that precious stage of life. You want it back.

Another reason may be that you want proof or validation that you love and honor the people's lives from the past. If you do this, I'm assuming relationships are extremely important to you. You want to keep those relationships strong by having proof that you cared about that person or that stage of life. You look to tangible objects as that form of proof. The question you need to ask yourself is "what does keeping an object from that person or that stage of life prove?" If your mother used a walking stick and you kept the walking stick for the next 60 years, how does that equate to you really loving her? I know many of us have come to believe that is what it means, but I can't help but wonder where did we get that connection? How did we get that linked up in our heads?

Let me put it another way. When you think about your children and grandchildren showing you that they respect, love, appreciate, and honor the life you lived and the love you offered. You would probably prefer they prove that by living an honorable life themselves, by the legacy of principles and faith they pass onto future generations, by the contribution they make to mankind, not by keeping your walking stick forever. It will be easier for you to let go of things from the past if you'll imagine a conversation you have with your ancestors or posterity years in the future. Can't you just hear it now? They ask you, "In what way did my life impact you? In what manner did you put what I taught you to good use? What proof do you have that you took your relationship seriously?" You say, "Well, I kept your walking stick for 60 years." I'm sure they will look at you and say, "What on earth did you do that for? Is that seriously what you did after all I offered you? You kept my walking stick?!?" I guess what I'm trying to suggest is that you honor the lives and the time spent with your ancestors and children by doing things that truly mean something. Things such as the life you live, the legacy you pass on, the love you share, and the contribution you make.

Yet another reason you may keep objects from the past is you want to be able to go down memory lane and experience the feelings of nostalgia any time you want. That experience brings many people joy. Joy is an experience we all long to have. The question I want to present is this, "Is there a way to go down memory lane without keeping things in the form that requires so much space and maintenance?" What if you were to take a picture of the object and write a few lines in a journal to trigger your memory of what that object meant to you. You could keep a lot of memories in very little space. You could take it one step further and scan the photo into your computer so you have it preserved in a way that requires even less physical space. You would still meet your need of enjoying nostalgia and memory lane without experiencing the problem of having too much clutter and too many things to maintain. Ask yourself, "What need does the object fulfill that a picture of the object and a brief journal entry couldn't fulfill just as well?"

Finally, sometimes you keep objects from your past because it gives you hope of going back in time. We all know you can't really go back. However, mentally living in the past rather than in the present allows you to, at least mentally, stay in the past. Some people refer to this as being stuck in the past.

Are you a person who is stuck in the past? A person who is stuck in the past believes that everything significant in his or her life has already taken place. He or she spends an abundance of time reflecting on the good old days. A perfect example of this is the character "Uncle Rico" in the movie *Napoleon Dynamite*. Although Uncle Rico was clearly in his 30's he could only think, speak or continually act out a high school football game that occurred many years before. As a man in his 30's he was lonely, broke, and going nowhere. The only thing he aspired to was playing that high school game over again. He was truly stuck in the past. I ask you again. Are you stuck in the past? Would you rather look backward than forward because it is so much easier to reminisce about where you've been than to work through where you're going? It's not a very high quality of life. In fact I'll go so far as to say it's a poor quality of life because you go through life as if it is already over.

When it comes to dealing with objects from your past my recommendation is to keep one box the size of a produce box for each member of the family. Keep objects that are meaningful to you and can fit inside your box. Take pictures of all other objects from your past. Write a few lines about that memory and what it means to you. Three lines are sufficient to hold the memory in place until you have time to sit down and write out a full journal entry about the memory. Writing less than three lines may leave you confused and forgetful as to why you wrote that down. There is a time and season in life for all things. Perhaps you don't have time right now to fully record your memories. Thinking you need to take the time to journal the memory in its entirety is just going to make you procrastinate getting rid of the object. Just jot enough down (about three lines) so you'll know what you were talking about when you read that entry years from now. You can journal your memories extensively when you are in that season of your life.

If you are technologically inclined, scan the pictures and journal entries into your computer. Make several copies of the computer disk. Keep a copy in three different locations. That way if something happens at home, you have a copy at the office, or if something happens at the office, you have a copy at your brother's or sister's home. Do what it takes to reassure yourself that you can keep the memories and your past *without* keeping the objects.

It's important that you do some real soul-searching and be completely honest with yourself. Come to terms with the *real reasons or issues* that cause you to hang onto objects. Those objects don't love you back. Those objects don't even know or care about you. The objects keep your life cluttered and overwhelmed. Keep the memories of the past. Just let go of the objects. I know this will be a difficult thing to do for some of you. You can do it. Honor the past by living an exemplary life in the present. Clear out the physical clutter so you can function at your very best, feel great about the way your space looks, and be able to maintain it in just a few minutes a day. You'll be free. Free to honor the past, enjoy the present, and make way for the future.

De-cluttering Obstacle #2
"I might need it someday."
Another one of the largest contributors to a highly cluttered home is keeping items, not because you are using them in your current life, but because you think you might need them someday. I call these items the "dreaded might's". A home is a place of residence in which people LIVE. If you are keeping things because you might need it someday your family is forced to

exist in a storage facility! You may think you can use your home for your family to live in *and* for storing the items you might need some day, but you can't. One of those uses naturally and automatically squeezes out the other. You are left with a storage facility by default. It takes a conscientious decision to reclaim your living space. Today is the day you set things right!

If, when you are de-cluttering, you hear yourself say or even think things like "We might need this some day..." or "We could use this for..." or "Yeah but..." or "What if..." beware! Those messages should send up a red flag that these are "might need it someday" items and should probably be discarded.

Before we go on, let's take a minute to address the difference between being prepared and keeping things because you might need them someday.

I can understand the desire to be prepared to meet the needs of your family. I believe that when it comes to the safety and well being of our families we should take measures for being prepared. However, I'm talking about being prepared for what your family really needs to survive: food, shelter, a source of heat, water, clothing, money, and possibly fuel. Just about everything else is small potatoes in the grand scheme of things. The items I listed are what your family truly needs. The majority of things you are hanging onto are things your family could use. See the difference?

Collecting or hanging onto items because your family might need it (what you really mean is they might be able to use it) someday is known as hoarding. Hoarding is a psychological and/or a biological disorder. You may be dealing with that disorder in one degree or another. If this is the case, you may want to work through this with a therapist to overcome this obstacle to having a clutter-free life.

Imagine, if you will, the worst-case scenario if something came up where you really could have used an item, but you didn't have it already stored inside your house. I'm not talking about the food, shelter etc. that I listed as needs for your family's survival. I'm talking about everything else. Would life go on as we know it? Would the sky cave in? Would there be options available to remedy the situation? Could you get the item somewhere else or do without it? If you seriously explore this I think you will find the worst case scenario really isn't that tragic.

Keeping a supply of food, a source of heat, water, clothing, money and fuel will help you be prepared for anything serious. Good insurance coverage will also help protect you and your loved ones. Getting rid of all the other "might need it someday" items will free up space for you to store the true essentials. It will free up space for your family to live and do activities that help them thrive in life.

Keeping things you might use someday also pertains to items you keep because you are **planning on doing a project or activity someday.** You may be hanging onto supplies to someday sew a quilt or paint the house. You may be hanging onto magazine articles or books you are planning to read someday. It could be any myriad of activities or projects you think you are going to do someday. Is hanging onto supplies for potential projects worth that heavy price you and your family are paying to keep those supplies? Consider the possibility that if you don't have time to do it right now in your current life, you very well may stay busy and never get time to do it. That is the thing about "someday." It's always out in the future, it's rarely here and now.

Keeping things you might use someday also pertains to items you keep because you are **planning on pursuing an interest someday.** You keep supplies for interests you have, but you are not actively pursuing at this time. All that stuff needs to go. If and when the time comes for you to actually pursue that interest, you can gather the supplies at that time. It will be far less expensive and time consuming to obtain the supplies when you are ready to use them than what you are investing in storing the supplies. Remember the financial, social, mental, emotional, physical, and spiritual costs you listed that you pay to store those supplies.

Keeping things you might be able to use someday pertains to items you keep because you are **planning to pass it onto your children or grandchildren someday.** Are you absolutely positive they will even want them? If they do, give those things to them now and let *them* live with the clutter of hanging onto all that stuff. You have plenty of things you are using in your current life that you'll quit using at some future time. You can give those to your children then. You don't need to hang onto items you are not currently using.

Let me give you a couple of definitions of hoarding.

1) The acquisition of, and failure to discard, a number of possessions.

2) Living spaces sufficiently cluttered so as to preclude activities for which those spaces were designed.

You may think the things are just sitting there not hurting anyone. The truth of the matter is that if you are not actually *using* something, you are *storing* it. And when you are storing things in your home, you can't use that space to perform activities for which that living space was designed. That is hoarding. Like many OCD disorders hoarding can come in different degrees.

I know some of you are thinking I have totally lost it. You may think I am way too extreme in what I tell you to get rid of. Never forget you are the one in charge. Take charge of your destiny. Do you want to stop paying those high costs you recognized earlier? Do you want to free yourself of clutter to the point you are able to maintain a clutter-free home in just 10 minutes a day? If you do, you need to get rid of all the items that fall into the "might" or "someday" categories. That will help you break free of clutter and chaos and hours of maintenance.

If you think getting rid of the things you've been saving for some future project, interest, good intention, or purpose is too painful, you need to recognize that your brain's interpretations of past experiences have created neuro-associations that cause you to *believe* it is going to be painful. Remember, this is only an interpretation. You can choose a more empowering interpretation – one that helps you break free of a cluttered life. All you have to do is organize your neuro-associations so they associate great pleasure with getting rid of those things, and great pain with hanging onto them. Once you do that, you will be able to easily let go of those "might" and "someday" things. Let them go. They are keeping you paralyzed and imprisoned. You deserve more than that. Let them go. It's O.K. to let them go. It's perfectly safe to let them go.

If you are not using an item in your current life, I strongly encourage you to donate it to goodwill so someone who will use it in their current life *can* use it.

De-cluttering Obstacle #3
Keeping objects that you love.

I'd like to address a comment I frequently hear. I am often told that I should allow people to keep all the things they love. My answer to that is I <u>allow</u> you to keep anything you want. After all, you are the one in charge here. However, my recommendations must strictly adhere to what will help you be able to maintain a clutter-free home in just 10 minutes a day. That is the grand promise I make to you. That is one gift I am committed to helping people acquire. That is what determines the recommendations I <u>must</u> deliver.

Think of organizing advice as something that comes to you on a pendulum. I give the advice that goes to the extreme left or right. I do that because people want extreme results and advantages in life. They want results such as being able to maintain a clutter-free home in just 10 minutes a day. You have to decide how far you are willing to swing on the pendulum with me. Different people are going to stop at different points. Those who have the courage to go the full distance get the full benefit. Those who only go a portion of the way get a portion of the benefit. Everyone (that applies anything) improves their circumstances, whether the amount of the improvement is great or small.

Here are my recommendations on the matter of keeping objects that you love. This also applies to objects you are keeping for sentimental purposes or to which you have sentimental attachment. Yes, there is value in keeping an object that you love. It brings you happy feelings, so it still serves you. I encourage you to find ways to *use* the objects that you love, so you can keep them and enjoy them. It's when you are not *genuinely* using them, but are just keeping them because you love them, that I extend a warning.

It's really a trade off. You can love enough objects that you keep yourself employed full-time paying for, picking up and putting away, cleaning, repairing, and maintaining those objects. This comes at the expense of using your time, money, and energy caring for, developing, and loving the *people* in your life. Surely you have heard of the wife, mother, and homemaker who didn't have time to play games or read with her small children because she was so busy cleaning house and keeping the home running smoothly. Or the person who constantly felt irritated or annoyed at his or her spouse because he or she didn't help enough in keeping the clutter picked up. Maybe that is a situation you know all too well. If it is not, you can take my word for it that it's a situation many people are familiar with. Simply ask yourself if you would rather bond with loved ones, meaning the people in your life, or loved objects?

Taking care of all those objects you love also comes at the expense of being able to do the *activities* you love. Some people are kept so busy maintaining their objects they don't take the time to figure out what they are truly passionate about. They never get around to deciding what they want their life to stand for and actively pursuing it. What are the activities you would absolutely love to be able to do but you don't have enough time? What is your grand mission in life and what activities help you fulfill it? What activities would make you feel like you absolutely love your life and you are so grateful you have the chance to live it. Do you have time, money and energy to pursue those activities or are all your resources tied up in collecting and caring for objects you quote-unquote love?

Yes, decorating your home with things you love is one way of using them. Just do this sparingly. It still requires you to consume your resources to take care of it.

By getting rid of the objects you love, you free up your resources of time, money, space, energy, thought, etc. to go toward your loved ones, your favorite activities, and your life's purpose.

This is the bottom line. Being happy requires a careful balance of surrounding yourself with people, activities, a life's purpose, and objects that you love. Some of you are experiencing the reality where your non-living objects are squeezing out the opportunity for people, activities, and life's purpose. My job is to help you take back control of your life by reducing the number of objects you are taking care of – whether you love them or not. You have to do this in order to free yourself to enjoy the *other factors* that will bring you happiness.

De-cluttering Obstacle #4:
"I really should hang on to this."

I am going to say or suggest things that you may resist or discredit. I know that, faster than I can form the words on paper, your brain is going to be searching its database looking for neuro-associations that pertain to what I say. You may have neuro-associations that conclude that what I tell you is going to lead to pain or something negative. Remember that your neuro-associations are merely *interpretations* of the realities you have experienced. You have the power to recognize your current neuro-associations aren't serving you well. You have to power to change them. Change them to support your progress in getting your home de-cluttered. Pay attention to your reaction to what I say and remember where that reaction comes from. It comes from your current neuro-associations which were formed from past interpretations. Not reality, just disempowering interpretations.

Another de-cluttering obstacle is that of keeping objects because you think you *should* be using them or you *should* hang onto them. I call these the "should" items. They need to be donated to Goodwill. Let me give you a few examples of what "should" items are.

Have you ever received a gift that you haven't used or liked that well? Perhaps you feel like you *should* hang onto it because someone gave it to you. Is that because you want to be sensitive to the gift-giver's feelings? Is it because you don't want to appear ungrateful? I encourage you to approach these gifts the same way you approach objects from the past. Don't create a misconceived connection between a non-living object and the love people feel who give or receive it. The love is there with or without the object. The object was merely a token of their love. It was an opportunity to communicate that love. Often in gift-giving the object has already served its purpose by the time the receiver receives it. It communicated love between the giver and the receiver. It does not retain the love between giver and receiver in and of itself. Letting go of the object (gift) does not really connect with letting go of the love between you and the giver. That is just something we got linked up in our heads somehow. It is an *interpretation* that keeps people imprisoned in many instances. Let me approach this from a different angle by asking you a question. Because of the neuro-associations you currently hold in your brain and nervous system, you have held onto gifts as a way of showing love and appreciation for the gift-giver. Am I right? Let me ask you this. Is there a way for you to express genuine love and appreciation to the gift-giver other than hanging on to the object itself? Would a heart-felt thank you card let the gift-giver know you were appreciative of the love they *communicated* by giving you the gift? Would giving them a gift in return express your gratitude? Be creative. Determine a way for you to share your appreciation other than keeping the gift if you are not really using it. Gifts are a common "should" item.

Decide what action you are going to take to express your love and appreciation to the giver other than hanging onto the gift.

Here is another example of a "should" item. Have you ever obtained an object that you intended to start using, but you never really got around to using it? Or perhaps you used it for a while, but than quit. I bet you look at that object today and think to yourself, "I really *should* be using that." But the truth is you are not using it. It is only a "should" item and it needs to be gotten rid of.

Here is a third example. Have you ever spent good money on something and used it for a while, but eventually you quit using it. Since you spent perfectly good money on it (especially if it cost a lot of money) you may feel like you really *should* hang onto it. Perhaps you are tempted to store it in your storage room or some other storage space since you are not really using it. Don't do it! This is definitely a "should" item. It needs to go. If you keep it, you are setting yourself up to spend money on it for the initial purchase, and spend that much money on it again paying to keep it. Two wrongs do not make a right. Two mistakes do not make a resolution. Don't convince yourself that you need to make mistake number two since you already made mistake number one. Truth-be-told you are only hanging onto that item for one of two reasons. The first reason may be to ease your guilt about spending money on it and not continuing to use it. You may even tell yourself you are keeping it because you might start using it sometime in the future. Let me refer you to where we addressed hanging onto items because you *might* use it someday. Get rid of it! The second reason is you want something tangible to show for the money you earned and spent in the past. Just remember for every tangible item you keep you pay a heavy price. You may think its just sitting in your storage room not hurting anything. The truth is that item just sitting there means that space is no longer available for an active storage item. An active storage item is an item you use at least once a year but not more than once a month. Your active storage item not using that space means it is being stored somewhere else which means eventually it infringes on your living space and on your day-to-day life.

4

Design a Plan

The "D" in E.N.D. C.H.A.O.S. stands for Design a Plan. This is the second step in the organizing process. This is where we take all that information you discovered in your examination and use it to shape the environment in each room of your home.

Start with a master plan

The first phase of your planning should be making a master plan for your whole house. Each room in the house is impacted by the other rooms. By sketching out your floor plan and determining ahead of time what you want in each room, you'll save yourself from some common mistakes.

One thing I catch clients doing is moving things into another room just to get it out of the room they are working in.

yndy wanted to clear out her kid's bedroom, so she decided to store kid's books in the family room. Then when she wanted to clear out the family room she couldn't decide whether to store the kid's books back in the kid's bedroom or in the playroom. She hadn't decided where she wanted a child's reading area. She just knew she wanted to clear the books out of the room she was working in. So she continued to move the kid's books from room to room, making no progress in getting her home organized. Over time, she moved things in circles, going from one room to the next room to the next room. This is a common mistake people make.

Creating a master plan can help you avoid that mistake. Decide in the very beginning what activities you want to have taking place in what rooms of the house.

Another thing I catch clients doing is planning for numerous activities to take place in a room. They don't look at the logistics of keeping all the supplies for all those activities in the room, let alone having enough space to actually perform all the activities.

Life provides us with numerous opportunities. There are so many awesome activities we could do in our home. Sometimes it is hard to accept that we only have so much space to store the supplies and perform the activities. Most of us have to pick and choose which activities we are going to have in our home now, and which activities will have to come later.

Only by designing a master plan, where we assign a reasonable amount of activities to belong in each room, can we be realistic of what will fit.

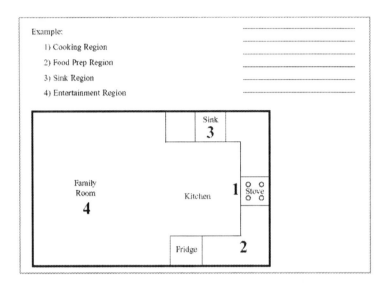

Assign regions on your floor plan sketch.

You'll want to create a master plan for the entire house. Free your mind of the things you have or the activities you have done in the past. Look at this as an opportunity to start with a clean slate. Look at it as an opportunity to design your home's organization by choice, rather than by accident. Make a copy of your floorplan that you can write on. Think of your entire home as your world. The first thing you are going to do is break your world down into smaller regions.

Place your regions

A region is the area where a certain activity is going to take place and where all the supplies for that activity are kept. For example, a family room might have an entertainment region, a reading region, and a game region.

I recommend you make a list of the regions you want in your home, number them, and then write the number on your floor plan at the location where you want to put the region. For example, having a cooking region would not only be in the kitchen, but right by the stove in the kitchen.

The typical home can be broken down into the following regions:

- Kitchen – cooking region, food prep region, sink region, refrigerator region, serving region

- Bathroom – grooming region, bathing region, toilet region

- Bedrooms – sleeping region, dressing region

- Home Office – computer region, paperwork region, telephone region, reference region, meeting region

- Entry – dressing region

- Family room – entertainment region, reading region

- Living room – music region, visiting region

- Laundry Room – sorting region, W/D region, clothes folding region, clothes hanging region, laundry products region

- Storage Room – decorations region, home improvement region, food region, clothing region, paperwork region, memorabilia region, less than monthly regions, outdoorsman region, etc.

- Garage – auto maintenance region, outdoor play equipment/sporting goods region, bicycle region, tools region, yard work/gardening region etc.

- Optional regions – exercise region, craft / sewing region, scrapbook region, art region, etc.

Refer to your examination. Look at your priorities, goals, and values to help you determine your regions and their placement. You're shaping your environment to support you in the things which are most important to you. Look at what you are actually using and where you use it. Your goal is to move away from putting things in a room because there is no other place to put them. Move towards putting things in a room because those are the supplies you need for the regions *in that room.*

Supply your region

Once you determine where to place your regions, you want to focus on one region at a time. The first thing to do is make a list of the supplies and containers needed for that region, or, more specifically, for the activity you want to have take place in that region. Anything that can store your supplies is considered a container, even if it is a dresser, closet, end table etc.

Since you have not yet sorted out everything you are going to get rid of, and since you have not yet sorted out every other room and brought the things into the room it will permanently belong to, it is going to be a little difficult to determine in detail what containers you will need. The sizes of containers you will need will change. The number of containers you will need will change. Therefore, at this stage of the game, only design the major containers such as shelves, filing cabinets, drawers, and baskets. Later, when you come to the Sixth Step in the organizing process, you can clarify exactly what containers you will want and need.

For example, if you were setting up your dressing region in the master bedroom, your list might look like this:

Region	Supplies	Containers
Dressing Region	Full Length Mirror	Closet
	Dresses	Dresser
	Suits	Hamper
	Pants	Shoe Rack
	Shirts	Belt Rack
	Skirts	
	Shorts	
	Socks/Stockings	
	Shoes	
	Underclothing	

Arrange your furniture

Draw a map of the space and sketch out ideas for rearranging the room to create each region. Measure your floor space and your furniture. Then, using your measurements, determine the best way to arrange your furniture.

In making your master plan, you will want to take into consideration the need to get a proper fit, have a comfortable flow of both people and process, the need to function efficiently, and your feelings while you are in your space.

Getting a proper fit

You want to avoid home gluttony at all costs. Getting a proper fit is a key principle that causes your things to stay organized.

Making things flow

When selecting homes for your things, consider both the flow of items throughout the process of using them, and the flow of the people working in the space.

For example, your laundry room needs to be set up so there is a flow similar to the following:

→the dirty laundry is sorted,
↓
    the clothes are checked for stains,
      ↓
        the laundry is put into the washer,
          ↓
            the laundry is put into the dryer,
              ↓
                the laundry is hung up or folded,
                  ↓
                    the laundry is put away.

The laundry should move smoothly from place to place, and so should the person who is doing the laundry. There should be very little traveling around the room while you are working on your laundry. Have the sorting baskets be within one step of the washer. Have the hanging rod be within one step of the dryer etc. Eliminate points of congestion and put in place what is needed so there are no breakdowns in the flow. Choose homes that compliment the flow.

Notice how it feels

If you like how you feel when you're doing something, you'll do it. If you don't like how you feel while you're doing it, you won't do it (at the very least you'll put it off for as long as possible). Pay attention to your internal feelings when you're in your regions or doing your activities. Make needed changes so it feels better. Have fun with it.

Make it fun

Organizing can be fun. It's meant to be fun. You just have to develop that fun making muscle.

Set a chair facing different directions with different views and see how it makes you feel inside. Then arrange the furniture whichever way made you feel the best. Choose containers that make organizing fun. It's the little extra touches that make all the difference.

Use your examination

Carefully go through your answers to the examination. Ask yourself, "How can I best organize to work with this?" Design a plan for how to work with your family's habits, style, priorities, and needs.

Determine your schedule

Finally, you need to assign a time for each stage of your organizing effort.

Activity	Hours	Day & Time
Categorizing	12 hours	Friday p.m. & Saturday
Hauling	1 ½ hours	Saturday evening
Assigning a Home	3 hours	Monday morning
Obtaining a Container	12 hours	Monday p.m. & Tuesday
Sustaining	10 minutes	Daily

When planning your work schedule consider this: The best way to approach this is to do one region at a time. Take one region of your choosing. Do all Seven Steps on that region. Make sure you have applied all Seven Strategies to cause it to stay organized. Then move onto the next region.

End result

Have the complete, detailed, end result in mind before you start the sorting project. All aspects of your Master Plan should provide this for you. Imagine yourself using this space after it is organized according to your plan. This will keep you motivated and clear in your direction. You are now ready to take on the C.H.A.O.S. and create the home of your dreams. Follow your plan and enjoy the results.

5

Categorize and Haul

T he "C" and "H" in E.N.D. C.H.A.O.S. stand for Categorize your things and Haul them to their destinations. These are the third and fourth steps in the organizing process.

Number one obstacle

The real obstacle to having an organized and clutter-free home is having *too much stuff.* Let me illustrate how having too much stuff impacts your life.

A new apartment

As a young adult I had formed the habit of lunging out of bed when the alarm went off, because I would otherwise fall back asleep and sleep for hours with the alarm blaring. At one point, I had moved into a new apartment with a new roommate. It was a one-bedroom apartment, so we had to share a room. All my stuff and I were shoved into my side of the room. The first morning in this new apartment, the alarm went off and I lunged out of bed – thump! Right into the wall! The wall wasn't on that side of my bed in my old apartment. I moaned, rubbing my head as I climbed out of the other side of the bed. As I got out, I stubbed my toe on something on the floor. I was whispering, "Ow, ow, ow," and remembering I had stuff in the room. So, I started sliding my feet when I walked so as not to jam my toe into something else. I started swinging my arms back and forth to make sure I didn't run into something. Sure enough, I knocked over a lamp, and got my feet tangled in its cord. I finally made it to the wall with the light switch, but I couldn't find the switch, so I started patting and rubbing the wall trying to locate it. Instead, I discovered – and knocked down – the pictures that were hanging on the wall. I finally found the light switch and flipped it on, and saw a person standing right next to me, staring at me. I screamed at the top of my lungs until it registered in my sleepy head that I was looking at my own reflection in a full-length mirror. My poor roommate propped herself up on her elbows and asked, "Are you always going to be this noisy in the morning?"

What we do with all this stuff

When we have excess stuff, we trip over it, run over it, move it, push it back, move it again, and we work and work and work to deal with it. I recognize that some people have a hard time parting with their things, but there is an irrefutable fact; you cannot have an organized and clutter-free home when it is full of too much stuff.

The 80/20 rule

The 80/20 rule states that of all our possessions, we actually only use about 20%. The other 80% are things we used to use or that used to belong to someone dear to us, things we feel like we should be using or should hang onto, or things we think we might use some day. I call these our used-to(s), should(s), and might(s).

Categorize

When you are sorting through your things, deciding what to keep and what to get rid of, ask yourself a simple question: "Why am I hanging on to this?" If your answer is any form of a used to, should, or might, that should send up a red flag. These are the things you should get rid of. These are the items which leave you overwhelmed, frustrated, and desperate. Get rid of these things, so you have space to keep the things which are important for your current life.

What happens is you keep these things, but since you're not actively using them, you put them in your storage room. That room becomes full, so you put them in the top of your closets or under the beds. Those spaces become full, so you put them in the cupboards, drawers, and cabinets. Those all become full, so you put them on the counter, windowsill, or floor. Little by little your used-to(s), should(s), and might(s) squeeze you right out of your living space. It's all being used for storage space. You have a simple choice: Either you can use your home as a place for your family to function and thrive in or you can use it for a place to store all of your stuff. You can't have it both ways. One squeezes out the other, so you are left with one by default.

Things don't love you back

You may love your things, but your things don't love you back. So get rid of the excess, so you can spend your love and your energy on people who will love you back. De-clutter your home. Work at it an hour at a time and little by little, you'll get the job done. If you can only do one thing that I teach you, this would be the one to do.

After you have completed your examination and design, you are ready to sort through your things and categorize each item as to whether it stays or goes. If it goes, categorize where it goes. In my work with clients, I have found that this process could take forever. I teach them how to Speed-Sort.

Speed-Sort

You will need five containers to Speed-Sort. They can be cardboard boxes, Rubbermaid, or wicker baskets. You can choose, but each container should be about the size of a produce box. Any smaller than that, and you will need to empty it too often. Any larger than that, and it becomes cumbersome to work in the room.

It's important that these containers be boxes, not bags. You want a wide opening so you can drop things into them in one swift motion. You don't want to have to take two hands to find the opening, so that it makes it difficult to put things in while you work.

Each container represents a different category.

Container #1 should be labeled "Trash." What goes in there is self-evident.

Container #2 should be labeled "Goodwill." This is for items that are too good to just throw away, but which you no longer want to keep. Some people have a yard sale. I discourage this, since it quadruples your work with very little reward. By giving the items to a Goodwill facility, you may write them off as a charitable donation on your taxes. Your tax deduction will likely be worth far more money than you could possibly gain from a yard sale. By donating your things to Goodwill, someone who will actually use them, can use them.

In our country we don't have a scarcity problem, we have a distribution problem. Many Goodwill facilities do more good than you can imagine. They benefit the lives of people around the world through their means of distribution. A blouse you donate may clothe a homeless or less fortunate person in your own neighborhood, or it may go to a third world country and bless someone there. They do such a great job at getting the right things into the right hands. I encourage all my clients to not divide what donations go where, but to donate it all to the Goodwill facility and let them use their judgment on where it should go. It makes the de-junking process easier and you can rest assured that they will get it where it is most desperately needed. So, let the Goodwill facility stay disorganized and quadruple *their* work by storing all your stuff. Chances are high that if you ever do need it, the Goodwill facility will have something just like it for dirt-cheap! Once I de-junked my home. I donated a lot of stuff to the Goodwill facility. Two years later I needed three of the things I had donated. I just went to my local Goodwill facility and purchased three similar items for a grand total of $6.00. That is pretty cheap rent for such an awesome storage facility.

Hauling them off to Goodwill is much less work than pricing every item, advertising a yard sale, setting everything up, spending all day at the sale, and cleaning up afterward. Plus you still have to deal with the leftovers, which you will probably end up taking to the Goodwill anyway. A yard sale can be a real distraction from your efforts to get organized.

Dividing your donations between family and friends can also be a big distraction from your goal of getting your home organized. Now you have a large pile of errands, favors, and good intentions. Chances are good those good intentions will never leave the house. Donate it all to the Goodwill facility and move on with your organizing project.

Container #3 should be labeled "Other Room." This is for items you find that you are going to keep, but they belong in another room. You don't want to take them into the other room while you are doing the sorting process. Think how much time would be involved in making all those trips into the other room. You would never get the job done. You don't want to risk getting sidetracked by something you see in the other room. That sidetrack could detain you for hours. Just put the items into the "other room" container until you are finished categorizing for the day.

Be careful that you are only keeping things you are actually using on a regular basis. Many people jump to the question, "Where does this belong?" without first asking themselves the all-important question of "Are we actually using this on a regular basis?" Your other room isn't going to have any extra space either. Every item you put into your "Other Room" box should be things you are actually using. They just belong in another room.

Container #4 should be labeled "Take Action." This is for every item you come across that requires you to take some kind of action. For example, a bill that needs to be paid, a library book that needs to be returned, a shirt that needs to be mended, a phone call that needs to be made etc. You are going to come across some things that need your attention. It may even need immediate attention. *Do not stop sorting or go off and take that action!* Simply put it into the "Take Action" container and continue with your sorting and *categorizing.* You will give those items the attention they require before the day is through, but you must also respect and honor your sorting and *categorizing* activity. If you don't, a job that should only take a few hours could turn into a job that takes several days. Stay focused!!

Container #5 should be labeled "Storage." This is for items you are going to put into storage. Just be selective in what you are going to store. Otherwise your storage room will overflow into other areas of your home and you'll have to start all over. Be selective!

Better Questions lead to Better Answers

You now have the five containers, and you're ready to begin. Pick up each item and ask yourself three questions:

- Are we actually using this on a regular basis?
- Is this something I would try to save from a fire?
- Which container does it belong in?

If your answer to the first two questions is "No," you should give serious consideration to getting rid of it. Make your choices quickly and move onto the next item. You should stay in one spot, pick an item up, ask yourself the three questions, put the item in the appropriate container, and pick up the next item. Each item should take seconds to dispense, not minutes.

Some people refuse to make the decisions quickly. They get bogged down in the categorizing step. They never get around to doing the next four steps. Life is better because they have de-cluttered but they never get to experience the joy of having their things be organized in a manner that stays organized. It continues to consume their time and energy. My recommendation? Make decisions quickly!

Your boxes will become full. The less often you have to leave a room to empty a box the better. When I work with clients we buy the cardboard file boxes with lids. We fill them and stack them against the wall until we have filled all we can fill in that room. Then we move onto the next step where we empty the boxes. After we are done the client can use the cardboard boxes for excellent access in the storage room.

You can choose to do it this way or simply interrupt your categorizing and go empty a box. But remember – the fewer interruptions, the better.

Let me summarize the pitfalls you need to avoid while speed sorting. Pitfalls that will make your categorizing activity take a lot longer than is necessary. Avoid asking yourself the wrong questions such as, "Do I want to keep this? Or Where does this belong?" Avoid getting into the distribution business. Just send everything to the goodwill facility and let them oversee distribution. Don't have a yard sale and don't distribute objects among family and friends. Avoid walking into the other room. Plant your feet and stay put in the room you are in. Avoid letting your categorizing session become a catch up session where you are catching up on a lot of loose ends. Just put those things in your Take Action box and take action on them later. Avoid putting things into storage that are not going to be used at least once a year. Avoid delaying decisions or making decisions too slowly. The quicker you can make the decisions the better. The more you hesitate or belabor the decision the more emotional baggage comes in that causes you to make poor decisions. Make decisions quickly.

Haul

After you *categorize* what goes where, you need to *haul* it off to where it belongs. It's important to remember that "haul" is a separate step, and should not be done until you are <u>finished</u> *categorizing* in that region.

On the haul step, we haul the trash to the outside trashcan or the city dump. We haul the Goodwill stuff to the Goodwill facility. Not to the garage. We haul the items that belong in another room into the other room. We haul the storage items into a labeled storage box on a shelf in the storage room. We take action on the "take action items," at least the ones which need immediate action.

6

Assign the Right Home

The "A" in E.N.D. C.H.A.O.S. stands for Assign the Right Home. This is the fifth step in the organizing process. You have made your examination, designed your plan, and de-cluttered your home. You are now ready to move on to the fifth step: Assign the Right Home for each and every thing.

If you assign the right home things will be put away far more often. If you assign the wrong home, things will continue to be left out, cluttering your environment.

This will greatly determine how much time you spend picking up your clutter. Assigning your things to the right home will help you function at your very best and keep your maintenance to a minimum.

Regions

The first home you provide is the home for your regions. Where do you want certain activities to take place? When you designed your plan, you should have assigned each region to a room in your home.

Furniture & large containers

The second home you provide is the home for your pieces of furniture and large containers. When you designed your plan, you should have decided *how* to arrange the furniture and large containers within each region so you could perform the activity in as few of steps or motions as possible. You drew it out on paper. Now it is time to actually *move* the furniture and large containers into their new homes.

Individual Items

The next homes you provide are the homes for all the stuff that will be kept inside your furniture or large containers. All the supplies needed for each activity belong within that activity's assigned region. But where *exactly* should they go?

Store it at the place it is first used

To determine the best home for each thing, ask yourself, "Where do I *first* use this item?" The first rule of thumb when determining the "home" for an item is also the third strategy that will cause your things to stay organized: Store things at the place they are first used.

Let me give you an example of this:

Mary's husband and children ironed their own clothing. They kept the iron and the ironing board in the laundry room since it was kind of a laundry-type item. The laundry room was the size of a wide hallway. There was not enough space to set up the ironing board in the laundry room, so while it was stored there, it was not used there. Instead, they had to carry it out to the first place there was enough space to set it up and iron their clothes. This happened to be in the kitchen. It also happened to be in direct view of the front entry. Every morning without fail, Mary's husband or children would go to the laundry room, get out the iron and ironing board, carry it to the kitchen, set it up, and iron. Every morning without fail they would finish their ironing and leave the ironing board up and the iron out to cool. Later in the day, Mary would see that the first view visitors who came to their front door would have was of ironing board and iron standing there. So every morning Mary would put away the ironing board and (now-cool) iron. Every day!

We asked Mary, "Where is this item first used?" We helped her recognize that even though it was a laundry-type item, her family didn't actually use it in the laundry room. We looked in the kitchen for a place to store the ironing board and iron. It was a challenge, as there didn't appear to be any suitable place. Finally, we hung an over-the-door hook on the door off the kitchen leading to the basement stairs, and hung the ironing board on that hook. When the door was closed, the ironing board was out of sight. We then cleared out an entire kitchen cabinet so there would be enough room for the iron to be set in it when it was hot but it could safely cool.

Now Mary's husband and children could put away the ironing board as easily as collapsing the board, taking one step to the door and hanging it on a hook. They could put away the iron as easily as taking two steps to the cabinet, opening the door and setting the iron inside. We made that change three years ago. In the past three years Mary has only had to put the ironing board and iron away for her husband or children four times. Compare that to doing it every day! The other thing to remember is that on those occasions when Mary did have to put it away, she could do it without having to carry it to the other room. It was much quicker and easier.

Do you store your games at the place where you actually play them? Or are they kept in a distant closet somewhere?

> When our client, Joan's, children were small they loved to play with their toys and games at the dining room table or in the adjoining family room so they could be near their mother. Picking up the kid's toys and games became a daily task for Joan and a major source of contention in their home. We asked Joan, "Where do they first use this item?" Storing the toys and games in their bedrooms, in the playroom, or in the hall closet was not following this strategy.

Joan invested in some nice cabinets with shelves and lined them along the wall nearest the family room and dining room.

Now putting away toys and games was a snap. There was very little traveling involved. It greatly reduced the number of times toys and games were left out. When they were, there was much less resistance and procrastination on the kid's part when Joan asked them to put the toys away. On the few occasions Joan had to put the toys or game pieces away herself, she was able to do it quickly and easily.

Store items at the place they are first used. It won't always be possible to store them at the exact place, but you should store them at the closest place possible. The easier it is to put an item away when someone is done using it, the more often it will be put away rather than left out.

Prioritize your items

To determine a more specific spot of where an item's home should be, ask yourself, "How frequently do I use this?"

- If you use it daily it is a "Daily" item. It should be stored in the most convenient location. This is at the place it is first used, between eye level to knee level, right up front so nothing needs to be moved out of the way in order to get it or put it away.

- If you use it once a week it is a "Weekly" item and the place to make its home would be at the place it is first used, between eye level to knee level, right behind the "Daily" items.

- If it's only used once or twice a month it is a "Monthly" item. Make its home at the place it is first used, below knee level, above head level or way in the back.

- If it is used less frequently than once a month it is a "Less than Monthly" item. Its home should be in a storage area outside the region, so it doesn't mess up the convenience of storage and use for "Daily," "Weekly," or "Monthly" items.

Store like items with like items

To a certain extent, you should put like items with like items. Organizing your things so they will stay organized and so you can function at your very best requires you make a slight adjustment.

Rosemary organized her books so all her novels were on one shelf; all her how to books were on another shelf, all her religious books were on a third shelf etc. The adjustment she made to follow the principle of assigning homes based on how frequently she used them was to assign one shelf for the books she referred to the most frequently, and to reserve a space at her bedside for the books she was currently reading (the books she was referring to every day). The bookshelf she reserved for the books she was referring to most frequently was in the most convenient location, and was filled with every kind of book you can imagine. Their only qualification to belong on that shelf was they were the books she referred to frequently.

Belinda wanted to keep all her spices together. We reserved one small shelf for spices A-F, another shelf for spices G-P, and a third shelf for spices Q-Z. Inside the cupboard door we put the most commonly used spices no matter what letter they started with. They got the most convenient location and were assigned their home based on how frequently she used them, not based on their name.

Having your things' homes dictated by where you first use them and how frequently they are used rather than by their size, type, or tradition takes some getting used to.

I have noticed while working with clients that they sometimes get a little paralyzed when it comes time to assign the right homes. They want to assign the homes according to tradition or habit.

It can be helpful to take the things into a different room. There sort them into boxes labeled "most frequently used," "frequently used," "occasionally used," and "rarely used." Then bring them back into the area and put them in their homes (cupboards, drawers, shelves, etc.). Start with the items that are only occasionally used, and put them (like items with like items) in the most inconvenient location in the area. Next, empty the frequently used items into the area (again, like items are with like items) and store them in a little more convenient location. Finally, bring in the boxes labeled "most frequently used" and put them in the very most convenient location.

I have learned to stay out of the persuasion or convincing business. It's my role to look at things with a pure perspective on how to minimize the maintenance and help you function at your very best. I make my recommendations and then allow the client to do what he or she wants. If you are uncomfortable breaking tradition on how to organize or arrange your things, that is O.K. Keep it the way you want it. It's your home and you should have it organized exactly the way you like. When the time comes you are tired of spending so much time maintaining your clutter, you can always come back to this book and work with my suggestions at that time.

Review

To make sure every item has its own home at the right location, first assign the region's "homes." Next, move your furniture and large containers to their new homes. Prioritize every item by how frequently it is used and place it in accordance with its priority. Be sure you store things at the place they are first used. Remember to check and see if the home for each item compliments the flow of things and if you feel good with it being there.

7

Obtain the Right Container

The "O" in E.N.D. C.H.A.O.S. stands for Obtain the Right Container. This is the Sixth Step in the organizing process.

Containers separate groupings and provide dividers, which help to keep our things organized. You want to make sure you choose the right container, or you may just be adding one more thing to the list of things you need to keep organized. There are a lot of containers on the market that look really cool, but in reality actually cause the house to stay cluttered. They add pain and difficulty to the putting away process and encourage people to procrastinate putting items away properly. If you want a clutter-free home, you must be very careful in your container choices. Choose containers that make the putting away process as easy as possible.

There are many different styles of containers. Containers can be:

plastic	big	fancy	rectangular
fabric	small	plain	round
metal	deep	colorful	
wicker	shallow	subtle	
wood			

I encourage my clients to choose a variety of containers that will make it fun to keep organized. I usually steer my clients away from using round containers, since those waste a lot of space and do not work well with other kinds of containers, but beyond that, you should use whatever containers speak to you and fit within your budget.

Make sure there is a proper fit

Make sure there is a proper fit between your things and the container you're holding them in; and a proper fit between your container and the space where you plan to keep it. If the container is too small to contain all of the items you are storing in it, it won't help you. If the container is too small or too big for the shelf, drawer, or space where it will be kept, it only adds to your disorganization.

Measure the size of the contents and the size of the shelf where the container will be kept before you go to the store. If you purchase a container and take it home, only to find it's not quite the right size, you are far more likely to just keep it and do the best you can with it. Returning it and finding the right container is a pain and a hassle. In very little time, that container will become one more thing for you to move out of the way when you are looking for something. It will become one more thing for you to try to keep organized.

Make it easy to put things away

Make sure it's a little easier to put a thing away than it is to get it out. In choosing a container, you want to look for one that makes it easy to put things away. Containers that are not clear and easy to see through, are awkward shapes and sizes, or have lids that are difficult to manage, all contribute to making it difficult to put things away.

Having a comfortably-sized target also determines how easy or difficult it is to put an item away. If you have to squeeze an item into a small hole, or wedge it into a tight place, you will find yourself resorting to just lying it down "for now" instead of putting it away. Make sure the target is a comfortable size.

Eliminate extra steps

Eliminate any extra steps in the putting away process. Leaving an item out takes one swift motion. That motion is little more than straightening your arm as you let it drop to the floor, counter, table etc. Since it is human nature to take the path of least resistance, you want the putting away process to be as close to one swift motion as you can. When it is just as easy to put something away as it is to leave it out, it increases the chances that people will go ahead and put it away. Look for containers that help you put things away in one swift motion. Or at least in as few motions as possible.

Label

LABEL!

LABEL!

LABEL!

When I first learned about the practice of labeling every "home," I really resisted. I thought it would make my house look tacky. So I tried an experiment to find out for myself if it really made that much difference. I organized things like toys, books, pantry items, and drawers. I used all the principles I had learned thus far, but I only labeled half of the homes. I lived with this for a while and documented my findings. I found I had to reorganize the items that didn't have their homes labeled twelve times as often as the items that had their homes labeled. I invested in a label maker, labeled the rest of the "homes," and have spent far less time maintaining my systems.

Do you remember that I said that everyone knowing where an item belongs contributes to items staying organized? Labeling is one of the best methods to help everyone in the family know where items belong. The more specific you get the better.

Staying on track

My husband and I go to the gym to exercise every morning. One morning we were on the treadmills. He looked over at me and said, just a little too loudly, "Man, you are beautiful!" No sooner had the words left his mouth than he lost his footing and went flying off the back end of the treadmill, landing in a heap. Everyone in the cardiovascular room heard what he said and saw what happened. It may have been embarrassing for my husband, but it was one of the most flattering things he's ever done for me.

He shifted his focus for just a second and it caused him to loose his footing. He landed in a heap. That is very similar to what happens when we organize. When we organize our stuff, as long as we are very focused on keeping things organized, we go along all right. Then life happens and something else takes our focus. When we shift our focus, we fall off track and our organization unravels quickly, we loose our organization footing and everything lands in a heap. Labeling where things go helps us stay on track, even when life is requiring our focus elsewhere.

Label your containers. Also label the shelf, drawer or space where the container belongs.

Go on "automatic pilot"

When you label the containers and the spots where they belong, things get put back in the same place – *every time*. When things are always put back in the exact same place you can "go on automatic pilot" when putting things down or away. You don't have to think about where it goes or look for its container – you can put it away automatically. And so can every member of your family.

Having clearly labeled homes creates a circumstance similar to walking by a puzzle that is finished except for one last piece. You are drawn to pick up that last piece and put it in the space where it belongs. When members of your family see labels and something is in the wrong place, they are drawn to fix it and put things where they belong. Everyone is capable of seeing something in the wrong place and leaving it there, but if it is labeled, it will increase the number of times your family helps you put things in the place it belongs. It won't happen every time, but it will happen often enough to make it worth buying your labeler and taking the time to label everything.

It is easier to recruit help in keeping your systems organized if where everything belongs is clearly marked. You can assign little Johnny to straighten a closet/shelf/drawer and he can leave it in the right condition, since everything was labeled.

8

Sustain Your Systems

The "S" in E.N.D. C.H.A.O.S. stands for Sustain Your Systems. This is the seventh and final step in the organizing process. Daily maintenance is required to sustain the areas you have organized.

If you have the Seven Strategies in place, your daily maintenance should be minimal, but you'll still need to walk through your home, looking for things that are out of place, and quickly putting them back in place.

Let's review the Seven Strategies:

1) Do all Seven Steps of the organizing process.

2) Maintain a proper fit between your things and the containers you are putting them in and between your containers and the space where you are putting the containers.

3) Store everything at the place it is first used inside its region, and within arms reach.

4) Make it easier to put things away than it is to get them out.

5) Eliminate extra steps in the putting away process.

6) Label everything.

7) Maintain it daily.

Again I say: Daily maintenance is required to sustain the areas you have organized. If you have the Seven Strategies in place, your daily maintenance should be minimal, but you'll still need to walk through your home looking for things that are out of place, and quickly putting them back in place. If you do it daily, you will be able to maintain your home in just 10 minutes a day.

Set up what I call the "10-Minute Sweep." Once a day announce to the family that it's time for the "10-Minute Sweep." Set the timer for 10 minutes and have everyone go to work as fast as they can to straighten up anything that is out of place. If items are stored right at the place they are left out, and if you are able to put things away in one swift motion, you should be able to sweep through each room in just a minute or two.

You won't be able to do every room in the house in just 10 minutes. You will be able to do all the main living areas plus one or two extra rooms one day. Then do all the main living areas plus a different room or two the next day. By doing this you are able to keep up on the entire home in just 10 minutes a day.

It's critical that you honor the 10-minute timer. *When it rings, you are through tidying up for the day.* If you try to make the family work "just a little longer," you will lose their cooperation in the future. Set the timer and honor when it rings.

There will be a transition period from when you first start to organize your home using the Seven Strategies to when the entire home is transformed. During that transition period, set the timer for 10 minutes and then *only* straighten up the rooms that have been transformed and have the Seven Strategies in place. For the rest of the house (the part you haven't yet applied the Seven Strategies to), clean the old way. Just be very clear that the rooms you have organized are limited to 10 minutes. If you only have one room transformed, spend the full 10 minutes on that room. If you have three rooms finished, spend one 10-minute session tidying up all three rooms. Soon you will have the entire home transformed, and will be able to limit your tidying up to just the "10-Minute Sweep." Your family will love you, and you will love your new system.

There will also be a period of refinement. When you see things out of place, don't just put them away. Look to the items for clues about which of the Seven Strategies is not in place as fully as it could be. Make the necessary adjustments, and little by little you'll find that fewer things are left out. Especially note if you have to do any traveling into another room to put something away. Move the homes for things until everything is stored at the place it is first used.

Let me repeat this one more time:

Daily maintenance is required to sustain the areas you have organized. If you have the Seven Strategies in place, your daily maintenance should be minimal, but you'll still need to walk through your home, looking for things that are out of place, and quickly putting them back in place.

Maintaining it daily will keep your maintenance needs minimized.

9

Implementing the Steps and Strategies

Now, let's look at some items and processes to see the implementation of the Seven Steps and the Seven Strategies. The following are recommendations I made for different clients. They will probably not be a perfect fit for your situation, but they should give you good ideas as to how to approach your rooms.

We will look at the following rooms:

- Living Rooms / Entries
- Kitchens
- Bedrooms
- Bathrooms
- Scrapbooking / Sewing / Craft rooms
- Family Rooms
- Home Offices
- Laundry Rooms
- Play Rooms
- Storage areas / Garages

Living Rooms

De-clutter so your things can fit comfortably. Eliminate things you are not actually using on a regular basis. Remove anything that has nothing to do with the regions you wanted in this room, such as reading, watching movies and playing with toys. You should leave ample space to grow.

Arrange your room into regions – entry region, visiting region, music region, etc. Put all equipment and supplies for each region together, so there is as little traveling as possible.

Entry Region

A common mistake people make is to use their entry closet to store items other than outdoor clothing. The entry closet is really a dressing region not a storage space. There should only be items in it that have to do with getting dressed to go outdoors or getting undressed to come indoors. So limit it to coats, hats, gloves, scarves, shoes, or boots. To establish a proper fit leave ½ inch space between each hanger and only use 80% of the rod.

A common challenge that people face is their kids dropping their coats, shoes, and backpacks on the floor as soon as they get into the house. One option is to get a coat tree for the adult's coats and transform the entry closet into locker spaces for your kids. In the locker space the coat hook should not be any higher than the child's shoulder height. The shelf for the backpack needs to be wide enough to fit a full backpack onto it without squeezing it or manipulating it. The backpack shelf should be at the height the kids can just swing the pack and let it drop on the shelf without any extra effort. The shoe storage should be so they can simply kick off their shoes into the space. If they have to bend over to pick up the shoes to put them away properly they won't do it. Make the putting away process of kids coats, backpacks, and shoes every bit as easy as leaving them out. If you don't have an entry closet large enough to facilitate all your children's coats and backpacks you may want to invest in some furniture/lockers that can stand at the entry. The closer you get it to the front door the better.

An entry closet converted into lockers for kids coats and backpacks

Visiting Region

Arrange your furniture so there is plenty of room to walk around the furniture and so there are tables to set down drinks, reading material, conversation pieces and so forth. The floor space in your visiting region should not have more than 80% of the space consumed by furniture, decorations, or objects. There needs to be space for people to flow throughout the space.

Often family members like to curl up in a blanket while they are visiting or hanging out with each other in the living room. I recommend you get a hollow table that can hold blankets or a large wicker basket to stand in the corner so you can store the blankets at the place they are first used. That way the blankets are not left out to clutter your space but are available to enjoy.

One option for storing blankets at the place they are first used.

Music Region

Pianos or other musical instruments are often in the main living room. It is important that you invest in good storage for your instruments, sheet music, and other equipment. I recommend keeping your music region in a separate room than the entertainment region, since piano practice may conflict with another person watching their favorite television show. Simply follow the general recommendations to de-clutter, arrange, and contain to establish your music region.

Family Rooms

De-clutter so your things can fit comfortably. Eliminate things you are not actually using on a regular basis. Remove anything that has nothing to do with the regions you wanted in this room, such as reading, watching movies and playing with toys. You should leave ample space to grow.

Arrange your room into regions – Entertainment region, Reading region, and so forth. Put all equipment and supplies for each region together, so there is as little traveling as possible.

Entertainment Region

Move your video storage near the television, so the videos are stored at the place they are first used. Invest in a video cabinet that meets the dimensions of the space available near the television, maintaining a proper fit between both the space near the television and the video cabinet and a proper fit between the video cabinet and the number of videos you store in it. Put like videos with like videos. Keep your animated videos together, other kid's videos together, instructional videos together, religious videos together, comedies together etc. Keep the most convenient shelf for your most frequently watched videos. Label the shelves where the different categories belong.

Reading Region

Position your reading chair and lamp near the bookcases in the corner of the room, preferably in an arrangement so that when you stand up from the chair you can reach the shelves of the bookcase without taking more than one or two steps.

Put like books with like books. Keep all your home management books together; family relationship books together, financial management books together, novels together, reference books together etc.

Keep a magazine organizer for each magazine you subscribe to. As the organizer gets full, toss out the oldest issue to make room for the latest issue. If you rarely go back and look at old issues, keep one magazine organizer to hold the latest issue of all your magazines and toss out the old issues.

Keep a tray or other container on the bottom shelf of the bookshelf to hold the newspaper as it is read and left behind. Clean it out regularly.

For young children's books, get a basket or container that allows you to stack the books so all the covers are facing the front. This way your young children, who cannot read the spines, can flip through the books looking at the pictures on the front cover to help them select the book they want. Storing the children's books this way will keep them from pulling out all the books so they can see the covers, and leaving the books all over the floor.

Use the most convenient shelf for the books you tend to refer to the most often. It will become your "top 20" shelf that provides you with the best access for the books you refer to the most frequently.

Label the shelves with the categories of books where each category belongs. This will help you continue to put books back in the exact same place every time and be able to find the books you need in a fraction of the time.

Organizing Your CDs

(Reprinted from the Organize Enterprise newsletter)

Okay, I want you to be truthful. Do you have a stack of CDs somewhere that have not been properly returned to their cases?

For years I had a neat row of CD cases lining the shelf. I even had the shelves labeled of where the different categories of CDs belonged. In front of the neatly placed empty cases was a stack of CDs four inches high. The CDs were out of their cases and piled on top of

---

each other. They were waiting for someone to match them up with their cases and put them on the shelf where they really belonged.

Does that sound familiar?

Here is a suggestion that will eliminate that problem entirely. Get rid of the cases they came in. Throw them away. Buy slim jewel cases with clear fronts. Buy them in bulk. Put every CD in a clear slim jewel case. The top of each CD is usually labeled, and when inserted properly the label is displayed in the front cover of the clear jewel case. If they are not labeled, use a marker to identify the CD by writing on the top of the CD.

Buy CD organizers that organize the CDs so they are front facing. The CD organizers look like an empty box with no dividers of any kind. You simply set your CDs in them so the front of the jewel case is facing you. You put 20+ CDs in front of each other.

CD Organizer

You need to watch the measurements of these CD organizers. Make sure they will be a proper fit with the shelves you are going to put them on. Get enough of these CD organizers that you have one for each type or category of CDs. For example you may have a different organizer for rock and roll, country, jazz, books on CD, talk tapes, etc. Label the organizers according to the category of CDs they hold. Get one extra organizer to hold empty slim jewel cases. Label the empty jewel case organizer "Empty Cases."

Insert all of the CDs into the clear jewel cases so the label on the top of the CD is displayed in the front of the jewel case. Put all your country western music CDs in the organizer labeled "Country." Put them in so they are all facing the front. Put all the rock and roll music CDs in the organizer labeled "Rock & Roll." Continue this process until all of your CDs have a home in one of the organizers. Keep 10-20 empty cases in the "Empty Cases" organizer.

It is important that each CD organizer is only about 80% full. You need to leave enough space in each organizer that you can flip each individual CD forward and see the label of the CD behind it. If your organizers are too full you have two options. Get rid of enough of the CDs until you obtain a proper fit or get another organizer for that category.

Give the organizers a home on a shelf or space that is below eye level. You need to be able to look down at them in order to get a full view of the labels. They should be located within arms reach of the CD player. Label the organizers. Place matching labels on the shelves where each organizer is to be stored. That way the same organizer gets put back in the exact same place every time. Now every member of the family can go on automatic pilot. They can know where the different categories can be found without looking for them.

Here is the "Putting Away" Process...

You eject a CD from the CD player. You no longer need to find the correct case to put it away properly. All cases are exactly the same. You pull an empty jewel case out of the "Empty Cases" organizer and insert your CD into the jewel case. You set the jewel case which now has the CD in it into the organizer holding its category. If it's country music you put it in the front of the "Country" organizer. If it's rock you put it in the front of the "Rock & Roll" organizer. You do not put the CDs in any order.

You just set them in the front of the organizer its category belongs in. Be sure they are facing the front.

Here is the "Getting Them Out" Process...

You approach your CD organizers. You go to the organizer holding the category of music you want to listen to. You start at the front and flip through the CDs flipping each jewel case forward as you go. All the cases are facing the front so you can easily read the labels of each CD. You find the CD you want. You take it out of the jewel case. You put the empty jewel case in the front of the "Empty Cases" organizer. You insert the CD into the CD player. You enjoy your music.

This system insists on a proper fit, stores items at the place they are first used, makes it easier to put it away than it is to get it out, eliminates extra motions in the putting away process, and uses labels properly. It will minimize the clutter and the maintenance.

You can use this method with computer CDs, DVDs, audio CDs and more. If you treasure the inserts that came with your CDs, file them in your reference file.

When you obtain new CDs simply transfer the CD to one of the empty cases that is in your "Empty Cases" organizer. Drop it into the correct category organizer. Throw out the old CD case and the insert. If you must keep the insert, file it in your reference file.

*(For more helpful tips, subscribe to the **Organize Enterprise Newsletter** at www.OrganizeEnterprise.com)*

Kitchens

De-clutter so your things can fit comfortably.

Eliminate things you are not actually using on a regular basis. If your kitchen cabinet space is limited, eliminate duplicates.

Recognize that there are so many gadgets available today for the kitchen and cooking, that it's probable that your kitchen does not have sufficient space to properly store them all. Go back to the basics. See if you could prepare your food using only basic pans and bowls. Eliminate as many gadgets and specialty items as you can so you have adequate space to store the basic kitchen items.

The kitchen should be divided into five smaller regions for each of the five major activities that allow you to prepare, eat, and clean up your meals and snacks: the cooking region, the food prep region, the sink region, the refrigerator region, and the serving region. Your objective is to stand in one place and reach everything you need to perform the region's activity without doing any traveling. Setting up a region-based kitchen will accomplish three major outcomes:

- First, you will function more efficiently. You will not have to spend time traveling back and forth in your kitchen.

- Second, you will produce better results. The five regions promote better tasting meals. Eliminating travel reduces the distractions that tend to make you forget to add key ingredients or overcook your meals, and allows you to be a more attentive cook.

- Third, you will be able to maintain a clutter-free kitchen with minimal effort. If you use an item and it belongs right there at the place you use it clean up is easier. If it is just as easy to put an item away as it is to leave it out, you'll be more likely to put it away as soon as you are done using it. So will your spouse and children. On the occasions an item is left out and you need to put it away later you'll be able to do so much faster than you used to.

Setting up a region-based kitchen means you have to break away from the traditional way of thinking. You no longer store food in the pantry and equipment and other supplies in the cabinets. In region-based kitchens the pantry is used for whatever region it happens to be located in. If the pantry is next to the stove it is used for the cooking region. It stores stove top food as well as the pots and pans etc. If the pantry is closest to the dining table it is used for the serving region. It is used to store the foods that go directly to the dining table such as cereal and snacks. It is also used to store the dishes that set the table such as plates, bowls, drinking glasses, serving bowls etc. It stores the table cloths, the paper and plastic dishes etc.

Kitchens were not necessarily designed with activity regions in mind so you may not be able to follow these suggestions perfectly. There may be one or two spots where you have to cheat and just do the best you can. Work with the kitchen that you have, but try to come as close to a region-based kitchen as you can. The closer you come to a region-based kitchen the better you will function in your kitchen. Now let's explore some possible tips for each region.

Cooking region:

You should be able to stand in front of the stove and reach everything used for cooking on the stovetop without traveling anywhere. The only exception to this are the ingredients stored inside the refrigerator.

Tip #1

A basic list of what types of items belong within arms reach of the stove top includes:

fry pans	cooking spatulas	vegetable spray
sauce pans	wooden spoons	pasta
pan lids	large cooking fork	rice
hot pads	tongs	soup
cook books	basting brush	canned vegetables
	gravy separator	sauces
	potato masher	oils
		instant potatoes
		stuffing mixes
		only the spices that are used to cook on the stovetop

Tip #2

For base cabinets be sure to install roll out shelves. It will increase the amount of usable storage space in your kitchen. Most kitchens need to make the most of every inch of storage space. Roll out shelves will also make a significant difference in how well your kitchen stays organized. Without the roll out shelves you tend to put items in the front of the shelves and push everything back behind it. When you need something you have to get on your knees and scoot things around looking for the item you need. Items don't stay in their assigned homes for very long. You can purchase build-it-yourself kits for roll out shelves relatively inexpensively.

When we first moved into our home our base cabinets in the kitchen had two small doors that met at the center of the cabinet when the doors were closed. There was a center beam that went from the top of the cabinet to the bottom of the cabinet. When the doors closed they rested on that center beam. I wanted to install wide roll out shelves that filled the entire space behind both cabinet doors so as to use the maximum amount of storage space in the cabinet. The center beam was in the way. If I cut out the center beam there was a gap between the cabinet doors when they were closed. It looked bad. I cut the beam out of the cabinet and then screwed the beam to one of the cabinet doors.

Use roll-out shelves for base cabinets in the kitchen.

When the doors were open the beam was no longer in the way of the roll out shelves. When the doors were closed the beam was still there to make the cabinet look good. I don't feel comfortable recommending people cut up their cabinets. I'm just sharing that that is what I did and it has worked out nicely. The point is to think outside of the box. Don't fall into the trap of thinking you are stuck with your kitchen the way it is currently.

Tip #3

Only store the spices that are used for cooking on the stovetop inside the cooking region. Spices that are used for baking, other types of food preparation, or decorating, should be stored in the food prep region. Store only the frequently used spices on your most convenient shelf. That way you avoid overcrowding the spices. Store spices that are used less frequently on a little less convenient shelf. You have the option of storing spices in a drawer with a drawer spice organizer. There are spice carousals that can be attached underneath a cabinet if space is limited.

Tip #4

Transfer food into an air tight food container that is identical to your other food containers. If you think you don't want to bother with this I challenge you to compare the time spent transferring your food to an air tight container when you buy it to time spent working with the large variety of food in their original packaging every time you cook. You will see you save a significant amount of time by transferring food to an air tight food container. It is far more efficient if all the foods are in a consistent container. I used to not be a fan of transferring food. I thought it was ridiculous. Then I timed it. What a difference it made! Make sure the lid on the air tight food container is extremely easy to get on and off. Don't ever stack containers on top of each other. Label each container clearly. If there are directions on the side of a box or bag of food, tape the directions to the side of the container so you have the directions for cooking. Once you transfer the directions on from the first bag or box you don't have to bother doing it again.

Food Containers

There are air-tight food containers of all sizes and shapes. Stay away from round containers. They waste a lot of space in the cabinet. There are even containers in the shape of a slice of pie designed to use with your Lazy Susan cupboard.

Tip #5

Install drawer dividers inside the drawers to store your cooking utensils. Remember to minimize the duplicates and eliminate the specialty gadgets. If you go back to the basics and only use the basic utensils for cooking, you can establish a proper fit within your utensil drawer. You can allow for each utensil to have its own assigned home where it belongs every time. This will greatly improve your ability to go on automatic pilot while working in your kitchen.

Tip #6

A typical pantry often wastes space that is greatly needed in the kitchen. I recommend you tear out the shelves that are currently in the pantry and build shelves that are a perfect fit for the type of items you are going to store in it. If the pantry is located near the stove you would store pots and pans as well as canned and boxed foods inside the pantry. Build shelves that will allow the putting away process to take one swift motion. For example, have a shelf just high enough for a fry pan to slide into, than you can have one swift motion in putting your fry pan away. You don't have to stack it with other fry pans. Do that for all your pans. Have some shelves that are just high enough for canned goods such as canned vegetables or tomato sauce or paste to fit into. Store a supply of each canned good directly behind each other so each is represented at the front of the pantry. Have other shelves that are the right height for the food containers you purchase. You can create a putting away process that calls for one swift motion. This will make kitchen clean up a snap. My recommendation is to figure out all the items you are going to want to store inside the pantry. Install new shelves to create a proper fit for those items to be put away in one swift motion. You can literally quadruple the amount of storage space you have in your kitchen by installing better shelves in your pantry and installing roll out shelves in your base cabinets.

Food prep region:

Tip #1

A basic list of the types of items that should be within arms reach of the food prep counter includes:

mixing bowls	measuring cups	baking decorations
mixer attachments	measuring spoons	baking powder
blender	knives	baking soda
rolling pin	cookie cutters	baking spices
flour sifter	apple corer	brown sugar
cheese grater	mixing spatulas	chocolate chips
baking pans	salad servers	cocoa
cutting boards	whisk	coconut
		flour
		nuts
		oats
		pancake mix
		powdered sugar
		salad embellishments
		shortening
		wheat
		white sugar

Tip #2

You need to assign the food prep region to the part of the kitchen that gives you the most counter, cabinet, and drawer space. You will need power outlets. It's ideal if this space is between the sink region and the cooking region. Sometimes that is not possible, so just do the best you can.

Tip #3

Apply the recommendations for spices used in the food prep region. The only difference would be that you are storing baking spices or decorating elements in this region rather than stove-top spices.

Tip #4

Apply the recommendations for roll out shelves in the base cabinets of the food prep region.

Tip #5

Apply the recommendations for transferring food into air tight food containers for the food prep region.

Tip #6

Apply the recommendations for using drawer dividers inside the drawers in the food prep region.

Refrigerator Region:

Tip #1

A basic list of the types of items that should be within arms reach of the refrigerator includes:

Tin Foil	Ziploc bags of different sizes
Plastic wrap	Containers used to store
Ice cream scoop	leftovers (such as Rubbermaid or Tupperware bowls with lids)

Tip #2

Only keep the bowls of the size that will fit inside the upper cabinet next to the refrigerator. It's all part of insisting on a proper fit. Larger Tupperware bowls would be used more for mixing than for storing leftovers, and should be stored inside the food prep region. Only keep bowls that stack inside of each other. Get rid of the odd bowls. Get a lid organizer to store next to the bowls.

Tip #3

You store items that are used less often than once a month in the cabinets above the fridge. Typically these cabinets are extremely difficult to get things in and out of. I like to store my emergency candles and matches in those cabinets. That is the only thing I store in those cabinets but I store a lot of them. We don't use them very often but it is nice to know exactly where they are when we need them so that I'm not fumbling in the dark for them. At the same time, they are not consuming valuable space that could be used for storing items I use more frequently.

Tip #4

Inside the refrigerator, use the shelf at eye level for storing leftovers. When people open the fridge to look for something to eat, the leftovers are the first thing they see. This helps leftovers get eaten rather than left in the fridge until they are no longer good and thrown out. This also makes cleaning out the fridge easier, since all the leftovers are together on one shelf. This triggers a constant cycle of cleaning out the fridge. When that shelf is full, you know its time to throw out old leftovers to make room for the most recent leftovers. It keeps things from staying in the fridge until they are unidentifiable.

Sink Region:

Tip #1

A basic list of the types of items that should be within arms reach of the sink includes:

Dish soap	Water pitchers
Dishwasher soap	Potatoes
Trash can	Peelers
Trash can liners or bags	Frequently used medications and supplements (not the medications or supplements that are not being used frequently in your current life)
Cleaning products used only to clean the kitchen	

Tip #2

Traditionally people store drinking glasses near the sink. I have found that this contributes to clutter in the kitchen. If the drinking glasses are stored conveniently near the sink people tend to get out a new glass every time they want a drink. Soon you have your kitchen counters covered with a smattering of used drinking glasses. To avoid this I recommend you put a label for each family member next to the location where people get a drink. In our home we get our drinks out of the water and ice machine in our refrigerator door. I have a label for Russell, Christi, Trevor, David, and Erica on the wall closest to the refrigerator. When someone gets a drink, they put their used glass next to their label. When they want another drink later in the day, they can identify which glass is theirs and use it again and again throughout the day. The used drinking glasses are at a much more convenient location than the new drinking glasses. It cuts down the number of drinking glasses that are left out on the counter. At the end of the day I take all the drinking glasses and load them into the dishwasher. Everyone gets a fresh drinking glass each day. This eliminates the tendency to get out a new drinking glass every time someone wants a drink. It's just an idea, but could be helpful if dirtying too many drinking glasses is an issue for your family. I recommend you store drinking glasses in your serving region, since they are also taken to the table to set the table for meals.

Serving Region:

Tip #1

A basic list of the types of items that should be closest to the dining table includes:

Tablecloths	Dinnerware	Cereals
Centerpieces	Silverware	Snacks
Table settings	Paper ware	Canned fruit
Napkins	Plastic ware	Pop or bottled water

Tip #2

Apply the recommendations for the pantry, if it is found in the serving region. If there is extra space in the pantry after all the serving region items are stored, you can use the space to store kitchen items that are used less often than once a month.

A customized pantry in the serving region

Tip #3

Apply the recommendations for roll out shelves in the base cabinets of the serving region.

Tip #4

Apply the recommendations for using drawer dividers inside your drawers in the serving region.

Homework / Mail Region

At the location where you put and sort your mail and look at the papers your kids bring home from school, be sure you have both a literature sorter and a good-sized wastebasket. You can purchase a literature sorter at any office supply store. This way, when each and every paper comes into your home, you can do the first stages of processing your paperwork immediately with very little effort.

A paper processing center

The literature sorter needs to have enough cubbies for each member of your family to have one, plus a cubby for bills to pay and a cubby for papers to be filed. If you have a large family you can combine the preschoolers so they share a cubby.

As mail and other paperwork comes into your home, first sort out the garbage. Put the papers you need to keep into the appropriate cubby. For example, Mom gets a catalog in the mail. She doesn't have time to browse through it right now, so it goes into her cubby. Dad gets a letter from his sister. It goes into his cubby. Bills go unopened into the "to be paid" cubby. Statements and other papers that can go straight to the filing cabinet go into the "to be filed" cubby. Kids' mail goes into their appointed cubbies.

When your kids come home from school they often bring a load of paperwork. Sarah's book order goes into Sarah's cubby for her to choose her books. After the practice and game dates are marked on the calendar, Scotty's soccer practice schedule would go into Scotty's cubby. Homework, art pages, and other papers that are not yet ready to be thrown into the garbage or filed go into the kid's cubbies. Homework pages mom finds throughout the house can also be put into the cubbies – this lets the student decide for himself whether he/she still needs the paper and deal with it appropriately.

Any flyers with details about announcements or events will be kept in the appropriate cubby after the dates are marked on the calendar.

Basically any paper that comes into your home that is not yet ready to be thrown in the trash or filed is processed through this paper processing system using your literature sorter and trashcan.

Now, these cubbies only have so much room. This is to your advantage. This provides you with an "out door" that tells you when it's time for you to sort through your papers to see which ones need to be tossed out. At one of my presentations, a woman suggested getting a deep drawer for each family member so you would not have to clean them out for a long time. This thwarts one of the greatest benefits of having a paper processing system. Paper will come in. More paper will come in. Even more paper will come in. If it never goes out, you will eventually be overwhelmed, and it is then a monumental task to get it all taken care of. The literature sorter cubbies are the ideal size. They limit how much paper can come in before you have to stop and weed out the old paper or take some action on the papers that are in your cubby. The limited amount of space helps family members choose their most important papers and toss those that are not so important. Perhaps Mom's cubby gets too full, so this tells Mom she either needs to look at the catalogs or magazines or toss them out and wait for next month's edition.

If your counter space is limited, you may wish to use hanging wall files instead. This keeps the sorter units on the wall instead of on the counter.

Playroom

De-clutter so your things can fit comfortably. Eliminate things you are not actually using on a regular basis. Remove anything that has nothing to do with the regions you wanted in this room, such as toys, games, and puzzles. You should leave ample space to grow.

Arrange your room into regions – toy region, games region, electronic play region, and so forth. Put all equipment and supplies for each region together, so there is as little traveling required as possible.

Toys Region

The ideal setup for toys is to have them separated into see-through containers without lids which are then lined up on very sturdy shelves. There should be plenty of space between the top of the container and the shelf above it.

Proper Toy Storage

This allows you to put toys away in one easy motion, and displays toys for easy selection. Even if several containers are dumped out at once, sorting and returning them to their place becomes a simple process.

1) Get sturdy shelves which are deep enough to house your largest toys. Home Depot has deep shelves, both with doors or without.

2) Set the shelves up in your family room or play room.

3) Get see-through containers which fit the different sizes of toys. Do not keep or use the lids. This makes it easy for all to see what is in each container and eliminates extra steps in putting toys away.

4) Sort the toys into the containers.

5) Label each container with a written label and a picture of the toy(s) that belongs in that container. Now even children who cannot yet

read are able to put their toys away without mom's help.

6) Arrange the containers on the shelves to your liking. Remember, your youngest children will probably need the lowest shelves.

7) Now, label the shelves right under the containers and put a picture there also.

For example: For your child's Duplos, label the container "Duplos" and put a picture of Duplos next to the label. Also label the shelf "Duplos" (where the container will belong when it is put away) and put a picture of Duplos next to the label on the shelf.

Game and Craft Region

The ideal setup for games is using Rubbermaid or Sterilite drawers.

1) Count your games. This will determine how many drawers you will need. You will need one drawer for each game.

2) Purchase enough Rubbermaid or Sterilite drawers at any local Wal-mart, Target, etc. The drawers you are looking for are sold in three-drawer units, with drawers measuring about 3 inches high, 10 inches wide, and 12 inches deep.

3) Dump all the contents of a game (including the instructions) into one drawer. If the instructions are printed on the box, simply take the box to a copy store and have them copy, fold, and laminate them so they will fit into the drawer.

4) The game board will probably not fit inside the drawer. You can either set two of these drawer units side by side and lay the boards on top of

the two units, or keep all the boards together on a section of your shelves. Be sure to label the boards. With the game board closed, turn it so the folded side is facing up and label it in the top right corner. Now you won't have to open the board to see which game it goes to. With all the labels in the same place, it will make identifying the right game board an easy thing.

5) Label each drawer with the name of the game inside.

6) Do the same with puzzles. Cut the small picture usually found on the side of the puzzle box, and tape it on the front of the drawer. This will make it easy to identify what puzzle is in each drawer. Cut the big picture of the puzzle box and keep it inside the drawer. This will help you put the puzzles together.

7) Organize your craft supplies so like items are with like items. Keep the most frequently used items in the most convenient drawers. Label the drawers with the craft supplies that are inside.

8) Label the shelves where the different games, puzzles and craft supplies belong. This way the games, puzzles and craft supplies are always put back in the exact same space. This allows your family members' brains to "go on automatic pilot" so the putting away process is even easier. This will impact how often things are put away rather than left out.

Now your games, puzzles and craft supplies will be better protected! When you find loose pieces, it will be easy to put them away. Games will be played more frequently (which means less time spent playing electronics) because of the ease in getting them out and in putting them away.

Proper storage for games and puzzles.

You may want to have doors put on these shelves to hide all the containers; but if you don't mind how the containers look, you could just leave the shelves without doors. That would, after all, eliminate two extra motions in the putting away process. It's important that you like the way the room looks, so decide what you like best as far as looks are concerned as you create your storage system.

Home Offices

De-clutter so your things can fit comfortably. Eliminate things you are not actually using on a regular basis. Get rid of things you used to use, think you "should" use or keep, or that you just think you "might" use in the future. *Keep only what you are actually using on a regular basis.* Remove anything that has nothing to do with the regions you wanted in this room such as the computer region and the organizing your family paperwork region. You should leave ample space to grow.

Arrange your room in regions – such as computer region and family paperwork region. Put all equipment and supplies for each region together, so there is as little traveling as possible. (If you run a home-based business out of your home, see my book, *An Organized Life at the Office* for suggestions on how to set up your business files.)

Computer Region

Keep computer books, disks, CDs, paraphernalia, etc., on or next to the computer stand and desk.

Family Paperwork Region

Review the homework/mail region arrangement for the kitchen for the first stages of managing family paperwork. Set up a filing system for storing and managing your semi-permanent family paperwork.

Filing System

You can use this method for creating a system for your family paperwork. This sample filing system uses a 4-drawer filing cabinet, four sets of hanging folders (each set a different color), plain manila file folders, labels, file tabs labeled Jan-Dec and A-Z, and several blank tabs.

Dated Paperwork

One drawer is for everything that is dated. It has 12 files labeled "January" through "December."

Instead of having a separate file for every account (bank, utilities, telephone, school loan, doctor, dentist, etc.) simply put them all in the file for the month the paper is dated. Any bill dated in January would go in the January file. Anything dated in February would go in the February file, etc. Now when you pay your monthly bills, they all get put in one hanging file instead of each paper having to be put into a different file.

Most dated papers that you need to retrieve usually need to be retrieved within 60 days. You can usually remember if you paid that bill or received that statement this month or last month. So most of the time you only have to look in one hanging file. On occasion, you may need to look in two months' files to find it, but usually not more than that.

The only exception I have come across is receipts needed for warranties. When you purchase something with a warranty, staple the dated receipt to the warranty immediately. For a warranty to be honored, you have to provide the receipt, and you may need to find that many months or years down the road. We'll talk about how to store warranties later.

At the end of the year, sort out the contents of your January thru December files into three separate piles. The first pile is for trash. Receipts you no longer need, bills that have served their purpose and can now be discarded, and other trash all go into this pile. Any paperwork you need to save for tax purposes goes into the second pile. Any paperwork you want to save (for whatever reason), but that you don't need for taxes, goes into the third pile.

After you have sorted out the contents of your 12 months' files, properly distribute the three piles. Toss or shred the trash. Put all 12 months' tax paperwork into one hanging file in your fourth file drawer with your other year's tax records. Get large manila envelopes to put the third pile of paperwork you are saving. Label the manila envelope with the month or year it contains and keep it in your storage room.

80% of time spent dealing with paperwork is filing paperwork away. By simplifying the filing process, you decrease your overall time dealing with paperwork by 50%.

This idea takes a little time getting used to, but will save you hours and hours of filing papers that are never looked at again. It will eliminate that large "to be filed" pile waiting to be tackled.

Product Instructions

For the mounds of paperwork that come into your home as instructions, warranties, handbooks etc, set up an A-Z file. File these items based on *what you call the product*, not based on what the paperwork says.

> For example, Evelyn's vacuum paperwork said "HOOVER" across the front of it. It didn't say "vacuum" anywhere on the cover, but she filed it under "V" for "vacuum," because that is what she herself called it. She did not file it under "H" for "Hoover," since she never called her vacuum "the Hoover."

In very little time you'll have this drawer nearly full. Now that you know exactly where the handbooks and instructions are, you will no longer have products only partially operating or not operating at all because you don't know where the paperwork that can help you troubleshoot a problem is located. Remember to staple the receipts to the warranties.

Reference Files

You'll need a reference file. This is for things that don't have a date and didn't come with a product in your home, but that you still want to be able to refer to easily.

Ask yourself, "Under what circumstances would I look for this paper?" Label it as the first thing that comes to your mind. Then file it alphabetically. Do not put all the topics that start with an A in an "A" file. Give each topic its own file folder, and each file folder its own hanging file. Then simply put them in alphabetical order by topic.

Danielle kept her files full of talks, vacations, insurance policies, recipes, articles, etc.

Magazines

80% of magazines are some form of advertising or contain articles you care nothing about. Don't save old magazines. Instead, flip through them and tear out the articles which are of interest to you. Create a reference file in your filing cabinet so they not only take up less space, but also allow you to find the article quickly when you need it.

For current issues of magazines, get a magazine holder (they come in different sizes) as a "home" for the current issues. As soon as it is full, cut and throw out the oldest issues to make room for the new.

Tip: Many magazines are now available online. You may want to consider letting your computer be your resource for those magazines and reduce the number of magazines coming into your home, adding clutter.

Tax Records

The fourth drawer is for your tax records. You need to keep your tax records and all paperwork that documents your deduction claims for seven years. This drawer should have eight hanging files. You should have one file for each of the past seven years, and one file for the current year. Each year, when you pay your taxes, put your file full of this years' tax documentation in a file in the front of the drawer. Go to the back of the drawer and pull out the file that is now eight years old. Shred it!

Tips that keep your files organized

Use a different color hanging file for each drawer or for each category of files. Use manila file folders inside each hanging file. Label the hanging file and the file folder by the exact same name, word for word. When you need the information, simply pull the manila file folder out and leave the colored hanging file inside the drawer to save your correct place to return it. Since the two labels are identical, you don't have to think or remember which hanging file this folder goes in. Since the hanging file never came out of the drawer, the files are kept in the same organized order year after year.

Organized files with proper labeling

If your file drawer is on the right side of your chair while you're sitting at your desk, put *all* the tabs of your hanging files on the far left side. If your file drawer is on the left side of your chair, put *all* the tabs of your hanging files on the far right side. When you buy manila file folders, buy a box of all 1st position (all raised tabs on the far left side) or all 3rd position (all raised tabs on the right side) folders. If all the hanging file tabs are on the far left side, you want all the file folder raised tabs to be on the far right side. Setting your files up like this is called "straight row filing." By using straight row filing, you no longer have to hunt and peck to find the file you are looking for. You just scan straight down the row. When you add new files, it doesn't mess up your tab placement. When you toss out an old file, it doesn't mess up your tab placement. You won't have to check behind papers that are sticking up in case there is a file tab behind it. They are all in a neat, orderly row. This makes filing faster and easier so the temptation to procrastinate filing is lessened.

I personally like the Smead Viewable Labels (These can be purchased at most office supply stores. You find them in the file folder section, not in the label section.) They stick up an extra ½-inch, far above any protruding papers. They also have a label on the front, top and back of each label. The important view is the one on the top. Since the majority of your file drawers are below eye-level it can be difficult to view what the regular tabs say unless you get far back and very low so you are at the same level as the tabs. Smead Viewable Labels have the label across the top so your label is easy to read, even when you are sitting up to your desk in an upright position. These also make it possible to color coordinate your tabs and file folder labels with the color of your hanging files.

For any other containers in your home office, label the container. Also, label the shelf or drawer where the container belongs. Label each drawer with the file category in that drawer. You can get a professional labeling machine at any local office supply store.

Scrapbooking/Sewing/Craft Room

De-clutter so your things can fit comfortably. Eliminate things you are not actually using on a regular basis. Get rid of things you used to use, think you "should" use or keep, or that you just think you "might" use in the future. *Keep only what you are actually using on a regular basis.* Remove anything that has nothing to do with the regions you want in this room, which may be scrapbooking, family movies, sewing and crafts. You should leave ample space to grow.

Arrange your room into regions – scrapbooking region, gift-wrapping region, sewing region, crafts region, etc. Put all equipment and supplies for each region together, so there is as little traveling as possible.

This is a design idea I had for someone who was very fond of scrapbooking. She needed a lot of storage for all her scrapbooking supplies. You might not want as elaborate a set up as this, but it may give you one or two ideas that may be useful for your scrapbooking, sewing, and craft room. Remember this is only one idea.

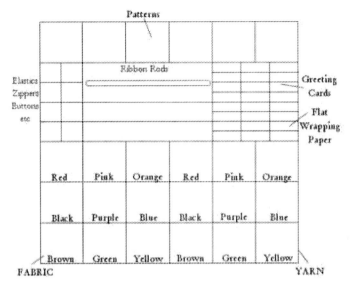

Sewing and Gift-Wrapping Storage

If you have one room dedicated for these purposes, and the funds to set up adequate storage for supplies, this is how I would recommend you arrange the room:

On the wall the door is on, set up a shelving unit to store your sewing and gift-wrapping supplies.

Divide fabrics and yarn by color. Keep them in the appointed sections.

Get clear containers to use as drawers for elastics, zippers, buttons etc.

Hang a ribbon rod and wrapping paper organizer. (You may have to do some custom building or focused shopping on the internet to find these useful items.)

A ribbon rod is similar to a toilet paper rod, only bigger. You lift it out of one side to add new ribbons or to remove old ribbon rolls. It's away from the wall far enough to allow you to reach all the ribbons. You can pull on the ribbon you want and cut off the amount you want to use each time.

The rolled wrapping paper shelves are supposed to be at a slant so you can see your selection and grab the roll you want.

Purchase a literature sorter from your office supply store for all your gift cards and flat wrapping paper selections. Organize it by category.

Literature Sorters

Across the top of this shelf unit is a place for all your patterns. When I organize sewing rooms, a common problem I run into is they are unable to fit the pattern pieces back into the small package they originally bought the pattern in. Here is another option.

Place patterns in 8½ X 11 manila envelopes. Tape the picture of what the pattern is for on the outside of the envelopes.

Group the patterns into categories. Then number all the envelopes.

Adrian numbered her children's clothing patterns

between 100 and 200. She numbered her women's clothing patterns between 200 and 300. She numbered her holiday decoration patterns between 500 and 600 etc.

Place the patterns in numerical order on the shelves designated for patterns. Label the shelves by category and number range where each segment of numbers belongs.

You may want to put a copy of the patterns picture in a homemade inventory book that lists the items by number, similar to those in fabric stores. That way you can sit comfortably and browse through your inventory book, until you find the pattern you are looking for.

On a second, windowless wall, you may want to build a section of shelves and organizers for your scrapbooking/craft supplies.

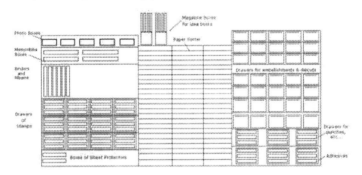

Scrapbooking/Craft Supply Storage

The far left section of shelves will need to be about 8 inches high on the bottom shelf for the boxes of sheet protectors. The next three shelves will need to be about 12 inches high in order to fit the 3-drawer units made by Rubbermaid or Sterilite (the same drawer units that were suggested for games earlier). You will use these drawers for your collection of stamps or other supplies.

The shelf above that needs to be at least 17 inches high for easy access to the large 12 X 12 photo albums. You may not have that size scrapbook albums now, but that is the direction the scrapbooking industry is turning. The next shelf up should be about 12 inches high so you can stack a few memorabilia boxes. The top shelf only needs to be about 8 inches high so you can comfortably store photo boxes for the masses of 4 X 6 photos you will collect and organize over the years.

The middle section of these shelves is just a large, 72-compartment literature sorter for your paper supply. On top of it sits a magazine organizer for your idea books, etc.

The far right section of shelves can be custom built to fit the specialty drawers for your die cuts and embellishments. (You can order these drawers in different sizes from *quantumstorage.com*.) of the size drawers you need will determine how much space you will need on each shelf. You will want the bottom few shelves to be 12 inches high so you can fit the Rubbermaid or Sterilite drawers there for organizing your punches, adhesives etc.

You may want to make an inventory book for your stamps, punches, die cuts and embellishments much like you did for your patterns. Number them and put them into the drawers in numerical order. Put an appropriately numbered sample of each in an inventory book. Then you can sit comfortably and look through your inventory book as you pick and choose what you want to use on your current scrapbook project.

Organize your stickers by theme and keep them in these small drawers. List the themes in numerical order in your inventory book as well.

On the third windowless wall, you can put organizers and shelves for your 12 X 12 paper and other supplies, as shown in the following illustration.

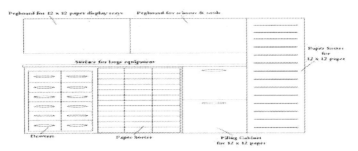

Organizers for Paper and Other Supplies

(We found Display Dynamics components from *jennycraig.com* to be particularly useful.) On the far right of this section we recommend a Display Dynamics Paper Station. To the left of that 12 X 12 display we recommend a Display Dynamics 2-drawer, 12 X 12 filing cabinet. To the left of that, place a 36-compartment literature sorter, and to the left of that two rows of drawers. You can decide if you want to use a Rubbermaid organizer, a wooden sorter, etc. You'll want to install a deep counter that goes over the drawers, literature sorter and filing cabinet, for storing your large equipment.

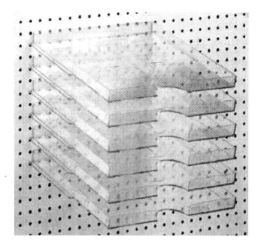

Pegboard paper trays for 12 X 12 paper

Above the counter hang a pegboard (available at any hardware store). On one half of the pegboard, hang Display Dynamics Pegboard Trays for 12 X 12 paper.

On the other half of the pegboard, hang scissors, tools etc. You may even want to include a "show off" area where you can display the latest pages you have completed to admire them for a while.

Sort your paper by size, color, theme, and specialty. Place in paper displays and literature sorters.

Sort photos by year, person, or occasion; it's your choice!

Label everything excessively!

Set up a worktable in the center of the room, surrounded by three walls of supplies. Now you can simply pull the supplies for whatever project you are working on to the worktable.

Enjoy your new scrapbooking, gift-wrapping, sewing, and craft room!

Laundry Rooms

De-clutter so your things can fit comfortably within your closet, cabinets, drawers and shelves. Eliminate things you are not actually using on a regular basis. Get rid of things you used to use, think you "should" use or keep, or that you just think you "might" use in the future. *Keep only what you are actually using on a regular basis.* Remove anything that has nothing to do with the regions you want in this room which may include sorting region, washer/dryer region, folding clothes region, hanging clothes region, and laundry products region. You should leave ample space to grow.

Arrange your room into regions – Put all equipment and supplies for each region together, so there is as little traveling as possible.

Laundry Region

If you have a small laundry room, have two metal laundry sorters, and your washer and dryer lining one side of the room. Have cabinets lining the wall above them. Put laundry supplies in the cabinet above the washing machine. Designate a shelf for each family member in the cabinets above the dryer. Designate shelves in the cabinets above the laundry sorters for towels, linens etc. Purchase a portable hanging rod to keep directly opposite your washer and dryer, or, if your room is too small, purchase a tension rod you can hang in the doorframe.

It is better to hang all your clothing other than socks and underclothing. (Review the Dressing Region/Laundry suggestions from the Bedroom organization section for details.)

Now you can do the entire laundry process with very little traveling. Bring in the dirty laundry and divide it into the laundry sorters. Pull out dirty laundry and stain check it, one garment at a time, on the top of the dryer before placing it in the washing machine. Wash it. Dry it. Pull it out of the dryer and immediately hang all clothing (except socks and underwear). Fold socks and underclothing and place them on the shelf appointed for each family member. Fold towels and linens and place them on the shelf designated for such over the laundry sorters (you'll probably deliver the bulk of the towels immediately after folding them). Each family member is responsible for putting away their own clothing that is hanging on the rod or on their shelf.

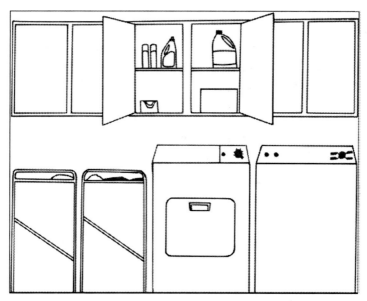

Set up a laundry room that improves your function.

Hanging all your clothing other than socks and underwear makes it possible for you to keep all the laundry inside the laundry room until it is delivered to the bedroom closets. It eliminates the piles of laundry spread all over the sofa or the master bedroom's bed. It eliminates baskets of laundry being left in every room of the house waiting to be folded or put away. It allows the laundry room to contain *all* the laundry in your home except for what is hanging in the closets or inside the dirty clothes hampers. Use laundry sorters in the laundry room instead of making piles on the floor. It will make working in the laundry room a much more comfortable and pleasant experience. It will preserve clothing better. It will make things flow rather than become congested. This strategy greatly diminishes clutter throughout the home because you don't have laundry strung all throughout the house. It greatly diminishes the amount of time you have to spend doing the laundry.

Bedrooms

De-clutter so your things can fit comfortably within your closet, drawers and shelves. Eliminate things you are not actually using on a regular basis. Get rid of things you used to use, think you "should" use or keep, or that you just think you "might" use in the future. *Keep only what you are actually using on a regular basis.* You should leave ample space to grow.

Arrange your room into regions – These may include the sleeping region, dressing region, reading region, etc.. Put all equipment and supplies for each region together, so there is as little traveling as possible. For example, you would put the small bookcase next to your reading chair, and the dresser on the wall closest to the closet.

Place items close to where you actually use them. Place them according to how frequently you use them.

Dressing / Laundry Region

I taught Marilyn how hanging up all her laundry would cut the amount of time spent doing the laundry by 50%.

It takes less time to hang clothing then to fold and stack it.

It takes less time to pull a dozen hanging items off your arm and set them on the rod then it does to open the pants drawer and put all the pants inside, then open the shirts drawer and put all the shirts inside, then open the socks drawer and put all the socks inside etc.

Because putting away hanging laundry is so much faster and easier then putting away folded laundry you experience much less resistance or procrastination from family members when you ask them to put their laundry away.

A child's dressing region

When a family member wants a particular item of clothing they can more easily see each item if they are hanging then if they are all stuffed into a drawer. You hear a lot less often the proclamation, "Mom, I can't find my shirt".

Kids no longer need to pull their clean clothing out of a drawer while looking for their favorite pair of shorts, only to leave all that clean clothing on the floor where it clutters the room, gets dirty from being walked on, and eventually goes through the laundry cycle again without ever having been worn.

To hang a sweater in a way that doesn't stretch it out or leave that funny little knob on the shoulders do the following:

1) Fold the sweater in half so the back right side is pressed against the back left side and so the sleeves are pressed together. For this illustration have the sleeves lying on the left side of the body of the sweater.

Hanging a Sweater: Step 1

2) Set the hanger on top of the sweater. Put the hanger upside down so the hook is just under the armpits of your sweater. The body of the hanger should be on the sweater, but the hook should be extended out under the armpits.

Hanging a Sweater: Step 2

3) Pull both sleeves of the sweater down in a criss-cross manner so they are now folded over the hanger and pointing out the lower right side of the sweater. You want the armpit of the sleeves to wrap around the point of the hanger where the hook and the body of the hanger meet. Don't weave the sleeves into the hanger, just lay them over the top of the hanger.

Hanging a Sweater: Step 3

4) Pull the body of the sweater down in a criss-cross manner so it is folded over the hanger and your sleeves. The bottom of the sweater is now pointing out the lower left side.

5) Pick the hanger up by the hook.

Marilyn found that her wire hangers got tangled with each other easily and made hanging everything up kind of a frustrating experience. She threw out all her wire hangers, and bought a large supply of white plastic hangers (10 for 88¢ at her local Wal-Mart). The white plastic hangers were easier to use and kinder to her clothes.

She hung up everything but her socks and underclothing. She hung up her pajamas. She hung up her shorts. She hung up her sweaters. She hung up everything. In her closet, Marilyn had one section with a high hanging rod for her long dresses and coats. She had another section with double hanging rods one above the other. There was a shelf above both rods. If she hung her shirts on the top rod, they hung down so low that they covered the shelf over the lower rod and she couldn't really use the shelf for anything. Pants that are folded in half over the hangers do not hang as long as shirts and blouses do. By hanging the pants on the top rod and the shirts and blouses on the bottom rod, Marilyn had space between the bottom of her hanging pants and the shelf below it. She was able to keep shoes all along that shelf. It looked great, and provided her much greater access.

She kept her socks and underclothing in the top drawer of her dresser. She kept seasonal clothing in the other drawers. That way her closet was clear of the out of season clothing.

She gave the clothing she could no longer fit into to her local Goodwill facility.

She put a full-length mirror on her closet door or a nearby wall, and her dirty clothes hamper inside or near the closet.

She kept the shoes she wore the most often on the most convenient shoe organizer.

She ordered shelf dividers from *LillianVernon.com* for the high shelf lining her closet. She stored extra bedding and linens right there in the room where she used them. She sectioned off a place for her purses and bags. She sectioned off a place for gifts and secret purchases. She kept an open container for dry cleaning, and another open container for mending.

She labeled each container, shelf, and drawer with what belonged there so items were always put in the exact same place. I told her to label on the inside rims of drawers. Label on the front of the shelves that are eye-level or above, and on the top of shelves that are below eye-level.

Sleeping Region

This is a simple region. Keep a nightstand by your bed to hold your reading lamp, alarm clock, evening literature and nighttime medications. Keep extra bedding either on the top of your closet or in under-bed storage.

Reading Region

Review the reading region arrangement for the family room. Do a similar, smaller version in a bedroom.

Bathrooms

De-clutter so your things can fit comfortably. Eliminate things you are not actually using on a regular basis. Get rid of things you used to use, think you "should" use or keep, or that you just think you "might" use in the future. *Keep only what you are actually using on a regular basis.* Remove anything that has nothing to do with bathing, grooming, using the bathroom, or cleaning the bathroom. Keep the bathroom closet free for towels and toiletries. You should leave ample space to grow.

Arrange your room into regions —bathing / showering region, grooming region, cleaning supplies region, etc. Put all equipment and supplies for each region together, so there is as little traveling as possible.

Place items close to where you actually use them. Place them according to how frequently you use them.

- **Daily use items** get the most convenient location (where you actually use them, between eye-level and knee-level, right in front).

- **Weekly use items** get a little less convenient location. (Perhaps behind a daily used item).

- **Monthly use items** get to stay right in the room, but in the most inconvenient place in the room. (Up high, or down low, or far in the back of your storage space).

- **Less then once a month use items** go to your storage space outside of the bathroom.

Divide your things so that like items are with like items. For example: Keep hair accessories together, oral care together, etc.

Get open containers that will

1) **comfortably fit all the like items,** and

2) **be a good fit for the shelf or drawer you are keeping them in.** It will become more evident what containers you need as you complete the sorting process. They should not have lids. Transparent containers are a little

better. Take measurements first, then go to shopping to find the containers that meet your measurement requirements.

Insist on a proper fit that requires one motion to put items away.

Label each container, shelf, drawer etc. with what belongs there. If there is a container, also label the shelf where the container belongs.

Never have a "Bad Hair Day" again!

(Reprinted from the Organize Enterprise newsletter)

You've heard of the bad hair day. The other day a woman commented that she was always having a bad hair accessory day. Hair ribbons, bows, clips, pins, elastics, combs etc. overwhelmed her limited space in the bathroom. Allow me to review a few of the organizing principles that cause your space to stay organized and how that applies to the bathroom cabinet with all the hair accessories.

Remember to insist on a proper fit. If you only have so much space you are only allowed to have so many accessories. The less space each accessory consumes, the greater number of accessories you get to keep.

Only keep the items you are using at least once a month inside your bathroom. Items used less often than once a month should be stored in a nearby storage space, not your living space. A bathroom is a living space. Become

---

aware of how many hair accessories you will definitely use over the next month. If you don't wear hair clips 30 days out of the month you don't need 30 hair clips. If you only wear a hair elastic once a week you only need four elastics. Hair accessories are sold in sets. The elastics came in a package with several other elastics. So did the clips, combs, pins, ribbons etc. Do you really need all of them or have you just kept them because they came with the set? The first thing I would recommend is to figure out how many of each accessory you or your daughters are really going to wear over the next month and only keep that many of each accessory inside your bathroom. Establish a proper fit by getting rid of the duplicates and the rarely worn accessories.

Store the accessories at the place you first use them. A typical bathroom has three regions. A bathing region, a grooming region, and a toilet region. The grooming region is usually set up in the space surrounding the sink and the power outlet. That space should only contain items that are used for the grooming activity. Let me share with you three different solutions we have found for clients over the years. Perhaps one of the solutions will work for you.

Pam needed to store accessories for herself and one daughter. She was able to use the drawers immediately surrounding the sink and power outlet to store the accessories. She only kept the accessories that she used at least once a month. In trying to create a proper fit Pam chose to use drawer dividers where she built the divider walls around the contents so all contents had a perfect fit with the size of the container/divider. The dividers came in 1 inch, 2 inch, and 3 ½ inch heights. Pam was sure to get the height that was the closest to the height of her drawers. She built the walls so the hair accessories only took up 80% of the space within the walls she built. That created a proper fit. A proper fit helps Pam maintain a clutter-free bathroom.

Melanie had five daughters and herself all using the

same bathroom to do their hair. Her bathroom drawers were full of other grooming supplies so she used the cabinet under the bathroom sink to store her hair accessories. Remembering that she should store items within their own region, she realized that towels do not belong under the sink. They should not be stored in the grooming region. They should be stored within her bathing region which was surrounding the tub or shower. Melanie realized that extra toilet paper should not be stored under the sink. It should be stored near the toilet. There are plenty of decorative toilet paper holders to store extra rolls of paper at the base of the toilet. Any additional rolls of toilet paper should be stored in a nearby closet or storage space, not her living space. Melanie recognized that the cabinet under the bathroom sink is in the grooming region and should be used to store grooming supplies such as her hair accessories. She installed a shelf halfway up the cabinet, purchased open baskets that were the right size for the hair accessories she needed to keep in them, and filled the baskets with the hair accessories. She placed them on the shelves beneath the sink. She was careful to leave enough space between the top of the baskets and the shelf above them so she could remove or return hair accessories in one swift motion. That way she didn't have to pull the basket out in order to get or return the hair accessory she wanted.

Lisa built a hair accessory center along one wall above her bathroom sink and cabinet. She could only have shelves that were six inches deep so she had to build several shelves and use little containers. She had to divide the accessories into smaller groupings so she could maintain a proper fit between her shallow shelves, her small containers, and her accessories. She was also careful to leave enough space between the tops of the containers and the shelves above them so she could retrieve and return the accessories in one swift motion. Lisa and her daughters had to use moderation in accessories due to their limited space. It was all part of living within their spacial means. They only had so much space to accommodate their hair needs so they only had the luxury of having so many accessories.

Be sure to label the containers and the place the containers belong so each container gets put back in the exact same place every time. That way everyone can go on automatic pilot and be able to put things away without having to look for the container.

These suggestions all follow the organizing principles of insisting on a proper fit, store things at the place they are first used, make it easier to put an item away than it is to get it out, eliminate extra motions in the putting away process, label and maintain your systems daily.

Now, organize your hair accessory center and then let your hair down knowing it will stay organized with very little maintenance.

(For more helpful tips, subscribe to the **Organize Enterprise Newsletter** at www.OrganizeEnterprise.com)

Storage Areas / Garages

The secret to keeping a storage room or garage well organized is to only keep the amount of things you can fit on shelves. This is a lot like the pantry. If you don't, you'll fill your storage rooms full of storage. Then you'll fill the garage. Then you'll store things at a storage facility!

De-clutter so your things can fit comfortably. Get rid of things you used to use, think you "should" use or keep, or that you just think you "might" use in the future. Keep only what you are actually using on an annual basis. You should leave ample space to grow.

Storage room containers and shelves

Each type of storage needs to be faced at the front of the shelf, and only duplicates of the same type of storage should be stored behind it. Label what kind of storage goes on each space of shelving so things are always put back in the exact same place. Never ever stack boxes on top of each other. Always invest in shelves and use the boxes like drawers you slide off and on the shelf. You want to clear out enough storage that what you have left can be organized properly and provide convenient access. Otherwise your storage room or garage will fall apart overnight.

Pull all equipment and supplies for each region together, so there is as little traveling as possible.

Arrange your storage into regions

Some regions for these areas might be:

Auto Maintenance Region	Memorabilia Region
Camping Region	Outdoor Play Equipment
Clothing Storage Region	Region
Decorations Region	Paperwork Region
Food Storage Region	Scouting Region
Gardening Region	Sporting Goods Region
Home Maintenance Region	Tools/Workbench Region
Household Region	Yard Work Region

Tiffany set up food storage regions: grains region, proteins region, fruits & vegetables region, household consumables region etc.

Jackson set up outdoor regions: sporting goods region, yard work region, gardening region, external decorations region etc.

Gather your supplies together after you are done de-cluttering. See what you have. Regions such as the outdoorsman, clothing, decorations, food, home maintenance, household, memorabilia, less than monthly, and paperwork regions should be stored in the indoor storage room. Regions that are used in the garage or outdoors such as auto maintenance, gardening/yard work, outdoor play, sporting goods, tools/workbench should be stored in the garage or shed.

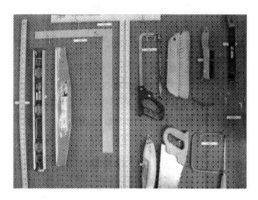

Tool storage

Buy or build shelves to fit the equipment and supplies that you have. Don't install a set of shelves and then not be able to fit your equipment on them properly. When you install shelves, be sure to maintain a 3-foot wide walkway for you to comfortably flow in and out of your storage space. Keep all boxes for each category together.

Storage containers and shelves for the garage.

Place items close to where you actually use them. Place them according to how frequently you use them within their regions.

- **Daily/Weekly use items** get the most convenient location (where you actually use them, between eye-level and knee-level, right in front).

- **Monthly-Quarterly use items** get a little less convenient location. (Store it behind other things, or on the floor where you need to bend over to get it.)

- **Quarterly-Semi Annually use items** get to stay right in the room but in the most inconvenient place in the room. (Way up high or far in the back of your storage space).

- **Less often then once a year use items** go to your storage facility off your property.

Get open containers that will

1) **comfortably fit all the like items,** *and*

2) **be a good fit for the shelf or drawer you are keeping them in.** It will become more evident what you need as you complete the sorting process. Unless you have a dust problem, they should not have lids. Transparent containers are a little better. Take measurements first, then go to Home Depot, Target, Wal-mart or the Internet to find the containers that meet your measurement requirements.

There are many Internet resources where you can browse for containers. Some of these include:

- Allbrightideas.com

- organized-living.com
- Organize-Everything.com
- organize-it.com
- shopgetorganized.com
- stacksandstacks.com
- target.com
- thecontainerstore.com
- Walmart.com

Remember, you are not limited to these websites. They are only a few out of many.

Label each, shelf, drawer, or location with what belongs there. If there is a container, also label the shelf where the container belongs.

Label! Label! Label!

10

Habits

uring the first step of the organizing process (Examine Your Situation), you took a look at your habits. I told you to work with the habits you already have. I recommended that you never organize your things in a way that would require the whole family to develop a new habit in order for that organization to stay intact. I cautioned that if you do, your organization is almost guaranteed to fall apart. I stand by that counsel. *However, I did not say you and your family need not develop better habits.* On the contrary, I think it is good to pursue constant and never-ending improvement of your habits. Always work on developing better habits, but when you organize your space, do it to work with the habits you already have.

Habits are fairly difficult to develop and even more difficult to break. I am so impressed with the power of habits and the role they play in how well someone stays organized. We all have habits. Some habits help us to stay organized (making your bed as soon as your feet hit the floor) and some habits help us to stay disorganized (leaving laundry in the laundry basket to be folded or put away later).

Organized people have a repertoire of habits that keep them organized. What we want to do is develop our own repertoire. The first thing we need to do to be able to accomplish that is assess our current habits. We need to see what we are already doing and, if needed, replace bad habits with better habits. Or maybe we already have good habits and just want to develop more.

Assess your habits

To assess your habits, walk around your house and look at the piles. The piles tattle tell on what habits you and your family have. As you look at a pile ask yourself, "How did this pile get there?" "What happened to create this pile?" At first I want you to only focus on the piles that you personally caused, created, or allowed. You'll begin to recognize some of the things you do that add to your workload. It's a real temptation to look at the piles throughout your home and cast blame on other family members. This doesn't accomplish anything. This only makes you upset at other family members. Stay focused on your own personal habits and work on improving them. After you have mastered those habits, and there is no more room for improvement, you can work on the family. The transition will take place more quickly and easily if you approach this with an attitude of making changes in yourself first. Meanwhile your family will catch on and gradually desire to improve their own habits.

Your family *will* notice the changes in you and your space, and they *will* catch the vision. I know you may not believe that at this point, but I assure you they will catch the vision. So look at your own habits and piles of clutter first.

Another way to assess your habits is to spend a few days watching your behavior. What do you tend to do first thing in the morning? Do you lounge around a while before you start your day? Do you get to work on things but neglect to do your personal grooming until later in the day? What do you tend to do, at say, 2:00 in the afternoon? Is your body screaming, "A NAP! I need to take a nap!" Do you feel spacey and unproductive or otherwise run out of gas? What do you tend to do in the evening? Are you still productive in the evening, or has evening become "off duty" hours for you? List the habits which contribute to your disorganization. Ask yourself, "What would be a habit that would keep me better organized?" Replace the habits that keep you disorganized with habits that keep you organized. How do you do that?

21 Consecutive Days

Research has found that if you do an action for 21 consecutive days it becomes a habit. I don't know the specifics about the research, but it is true that the brain seems to watch your behavior very closely. It hesitates to put an action "on automatic pilot" until it's sure it's a permanent change. Something about the 21-day time frame lets your brain relax and accept it. It puts the new action "on automatic pilot" where you do it without much thought or effort. However, if you miss a day, your brain says, "See, I told you it's not a permanent change. It's a good thing we didn't put it on automatic pilot." Then you just have to start all over. But, if you want to make something a habit, do it for 21 consecutive days and it becomes yours. This is how you become organized. Pick two or three habits you want to develop each month. Make a true decision to do them for 21 consecutive days. Remember, a true decision means you cut yourself away from any other possibility. Once these habits are yours, you can pick two or three new ones to work on for the next month. In very little time you will have a repertoire of habits that will cause you to stay organized.

The Seven "Duh" Habits

Because these next few habits I'm going to recommend seem like such obvious things to do, I call these my "Seven 'duh' habits for highly effective right-brainers." These are the basic habits you need *just* to have the energy and ability to *get* organized.

"Duh" Habit #1:
Get enough sleep

If you ask an organized person what time they go to bed they'll tell you, "Ten o'clock" or "Ten thirty". They will have the clock dictate what time they get into bed and go to sleep. If you ask a disorganized person what time they go to bed they'll tell you, "Well last night I was up doing laundry until one o'clock in the morning" or "it all depends on what's on TV or if my husband wants to talk". Their bedtime is variable. They go to bed at a different time every night.

The first "duh" habit you want to develop is to establish a set time to be in bed each night and then see to it that you are in bed with the lights out by that time. Have the clock determine what time you are going to sleep, not activities or pressures of the day. We know our kids can't function well without enough sleep, so we set a bedtime for them. Do the same thing for yourself to be sure you get enough sleep. Also establish a set time to get up every morning. Getting on a regular schedule, going to bed at the same time every night and getting up at the same time every morning (with enough sleep in between), will give you great stamina. Far more stamina in fact than if you get the same amount of sleep (or more) but with variable times for going to bed and getting up.

"Duh" Habit #2:
Eat the right food

Go to the grocery store on time. Don't let the cupboard get bare. Eat real food, not junk food. Pay attention to what passes your lips and try to make the majority of it be food that fuels and energizes you.

"Duh" Habit #3:
Drink enough water

Drink 8-10 glasses of water each and every day. Water carries oxygen to your brain. It will make a tremendous difference in how you feel. Water serves as a great pick-me-up in the afternoon when your body is screaming for a nap.

"Duh" Habit #4:
Do some kind of exercise every day

You have your own set of physical limitations and/or capabilities. Do whatever you need to get some exercise. This is not a health book, so I'll just say that exercise is required for you to feel well enough to really get organized. Choose an exercise that energizes you, not one that wipes you out.

"Duh" habit #5:
Pay your bills on time

You can't devote your energies to getting organized if you're kicked out of your home or your power or water is shut off. Pay your bills on time.

"Duh" Habit #6:
Do your laundry every day

Don't let it get behind. Keep it caught up. Trust me, you want people to have clothes on when they leave the house! You don't want to be thrown back into crisis management, so keep that laundry caught up. Do a load or two every day. Make it a habit to put a load in every morning and make sure the washer is empty every evening before you go to bed.

"Duh" Habit #7:
Keep your dishes caught up

Load the dishwasher every night and turn it on before you go to bed. It doesn't matter how full it is. Then, in the morning develop the habit of emptying the dishwasher so that dishes that are dirtied throughout the day can be rinsed off and put into the dishwasher.

Some Little Habits

Beyond the seven "duh" habits, I'm going to recommend some "little" habits that make a big difference.

Little Habit #1:
Shower, dress, do your hair, and put on
your makeup within one hour of
getting up in the morning.

This one was so hard for me. There are so many mornings when I feel like, "I don't want to be organized today, I want to be relaxed." But I'll tell you what. I have discovered amazing benefits from developing this habit. Psychologically speaking, I *felt* like I was an organized person. That became my identity for the day, because I was ready for the day at an early hour. All day long I would act in a way that *matched* that identity. So if I showered, dressed, and did my hair and make up within one hour of getting up in the morning I was organized all day long. If I did not shower, dress, or do my hair and makeup within the first hour of getting up in the morning, I *had a slacker mentality all day long.* My identity was, "I'm not being organized today," and I matched that identity all day long. Getting dressed all the way to my shoes sent my brain the message that I was ready to go to work, so I jumped into my work with more energy and enthusiasm. I also have to say that it is really nice not getting caught in my sweats with nighttime hair and no makeup!

If life is busy during that first hour, I suggest you get up 30 minutes before the rest of the family, so you can be showered, dressed, and well-groomed within the first hour of waking up. Just be sure you go to bed 30 minutes earlier so you still get enough sleep. If you exercise in the morning, at least be in the shower within that first hour.

Starting tonight, I suggest you determine a set bedtime for yourself and be in bed at that time. Tomorrow morning, get up at your set time and be showered, dressed all the way to your shoes, and have your hair done and your makeup on within one hour of waking up. Do this for 21 consecutive days.

Little Habit #2:
Make your bed as soon as your feet hit
the floor.

You're still sleepy and not even aware you are doing it. Even if your husband is still in bed, make the bed with him in it! By developing the habit of making your bed before anything else, you establish in your mind that you are being organized today. You may not be organized everyday, but you are being organized today. You eliminate that little irritation that hangs over you during the day that you haven't even made the bed yet. It really is nice to have one task done before you even go to the bathroom. (Although, there are some mornings I'm really fast at making that bed because I need to get to the bathroom!)

I say my prayers when I first get up in the morning. So I roll out of bed onto my knees (y feet have not yet touched the floor). I say my prayers. Then, as I rise to my feet I pull the covers up and make the bed. Try it. It works just fine.

Little Habit #3:
Don't walk by the clutter. Pick it up as
you pass by and put it away.

Remember that once it's a habit, you do it without conscious thought. Consider how much cleaner your home would be and how fewer things would be misplaced if you simply had the habit of not walking by the clutter, but picking it up as you pass by and putting it away. This is a habit you work on all day long, but once it is yours it makes a huge difference. Here is a happy thought: If you store things at the place they are first used, as suggested in the 3rd Strategy, putting it away will only take a half a second.

Little Habit #4:
Be a person who puts things away
when you are through using them.

You, yourself, need to develop this habit before you can expect your children and spouse to do so. Pay attention to how frequently you set something down or leave it behind instead of putting it back where it belongs. Develop the organized habit of putting things away when you are through using them.

11

Gaining Your Family's Cooperation

hen one of our children (who will remain unnamed) was two years old, we came to know how our children can surprise us. One Sunday when we were at church, we were taking the sacramental bread. Our two-year-old took his piece of bread, put it into his mouth, got it good and soggy, and then decided he wanted a different piece. So he tried to put his soggy piece back on the sacramental tray for someone else to enjoy. We stopped him in time, but it really made him mad. He started screaming and carrying on like only an angry two year-old can. I could tell that I was not going to be nurturing about this, so my husband took our angry child out of the church meeting. My husband was planning on just loving the child through this and letting him get it out of his system. He took the toddler into a small classroom, sat down on a chair that was open in the back, and let our son get down off of his lap. No sooner had my husband let him down, than our two year-old son ran around behind his father's chair and bit my husband right on the butt! My husband quickly lost the need to be nurturing. He said, "You little (blankety-blank)!" picked him up, and spanked him soundly. I laughed when I heard what happened, but I also felt great concern. We all know how small children tend to repeat the things they hear right at the very place and time that would embarrass you the most. I could just picture the next time the child needed to be taken out of the church meeting. He would be yelling at the top of his lungs, "No daddy, don't spank me. I won't be a little (blankety-blank)."

My husband was surprised when my son bit him in the butt. There are better ways to surprise your parents. I tell you this story to emphasize that if you make it easy for your family to keep things organized, and you teach and train them how to do it, they will surprise you at how well they can and will do. Hopefully it will be a more pleasant surprise than being bit in the butt. If you try to shortcut the training, the results will be disappointing but not surprising.

Make it easy!

Before approaching your family about maintaining an organized home, do everything in your power to make it easy to keep maintained.

- Examine your situation, and set up your organization to work with your situation.

- Be sure there is a proper fit between your items and the container where they belong, and between your container and the space where you will be keeping it. Avoid gluttony!

- Store each item at the point it is first used.

- Make sure things are a little easier to put away than they are to get out.

- Eliminate any extra steps in the putting-away process.

- Label where everything belongs.

- Set up daily maintenance.

There are many strategies that will help reduce clutter for the short term. The only way you will gain your family's cooperation on a long term basis is to make it so easy to put things away that they don't mind doing it. The good news is making it that easy is completely in your control. The bad news is you can't rush the process. You need to take the time to transform each region so all Seven Strategies are in place before you can expect your family to cooperate on a long term basis. This strategy is the main strategy you want to apply. It is the only strategy that will cause long lasting results and gain your family's cooperation indefinitely.

Once you have transformed your regions, get your family started doing the "10-Minute Sweep". The "10-Minute Sweep" is only for the areas that have already been transformed. You clean up the rest of the house the same way you have always been doing it. Make sure your family makes the distinction between the areas. Watch for items that are being left out and evaluate which one of the Seven Strategies needs to be refined. Honor the 10 minute limit. I know it will be tempting to ask them to work a little longer than 10 minutes but don't do it. You'll lose their cooperation from now on unless you honor the 10 minute limit. Remember you obtain clutter-free living by implementing the Seven Strategies better than you have been. You don't gain it by persuading your family members to work longer.

Teaching your family members to pick up after themselves

Here is a quick fix to help you gain your family's cooperation in putting things away when they are done using them. It's a short term fix so you want to implement the Seven Strategies as soon as you can.

1. Let them know that as the parent, you have the responsibility to help them develop as a person, including developing good habits.

2. Let them know that you want to help them by setting up what you call a "Supportive Maid Service."

3. Each member of the family gets a pint-size jar (or some other cute container) with quarters in it. You decide how many quarters, perhaps two, perhaps 12. Each family member is responsible for providing their own quarters. The parents can provide work opportunities whenever someone needs to earn more quarters.

4. For this example, suppose everyone starts each week with 12 quarters. If someone runs out of quarters, **all** privileges are suspended until they have worked enough to earn 12 quarters to refill their jar.

5. Whenever someone leaves something out, another family member may pick it up and put it away.

6. Immediately after the family member puts the item away, they may go to the jars, take a quarter out of the jar belonging to the person who left the item out, and put the quarter into their own jar.

7. There is also a petty cash jar full of quarters. Whenever you have an odd job that needs to be

done, you can ask, "Who wants to earn some petty cash?" Thus you get volunteers for your odd jobs.

8. At the end of the week each family member leaves 12 quarters in their jar, but gets to keep the rest.

You can decide if you're going to use quarters, nickels, pennies, or paper currency. Determine what will work best for your budget and the ages of your children.

When we first started using this method, our children acted like they were out to get each other. They gloated and rubbed salt in the wound every time they picked something up and took someone's quarter. We decided if they told anybody about the job done or the quarter earned, they had to give the quarter to the person they told. This helped keep a more pleasant atmosphere in the home.

If anyone complained, they had to pay a quarter both to the person that picked up after them **_and_** to the parent who had to listen to their complaining.

We started doing this when our children were young. We used nickels at that time. As they got older we found a nickel didn't motivate them very much, so we increased it to a quarter.

Your children will test the system and try to find new ways to defeat it. Simply put into place whatever is needed to make it work for your family. Instead of working for monetary gain, perhaps fun activities, or other treats would work. Each family is unique, and you must shape and mold this system to work for your family.

When selecting rewards and punishments, make sure they are things you really will do. Do you prefer money, time, or other rewards?

If your budget is a concern, take an expense that you usually pay for and make it their responsibility. The quarters will provide them a way to meet that responsibility, and reducing an expense you usually take care of increases your budget.

Bruce and Bethany used to pay for their children's clothing. When they started this system, they made their children responsible for buying their own clothing. Bruce and Bethany decided what articles of clothing had to be purchased at what times of year before the children could spend their money on other things. This created room in Bruce and Bethany's budget to fund the system by providing work opportunities for the children to earn their own quarters. This system provided enough income opportunity for the children to earn the money needed to purchase the clothing, so the new requirement was not beyond their means.

Jacqueline used the quarter system for a while. It gradually evolved into another system where everyone was responsible for putting things away after they were done using them.

Jacqueline established that even though she and her husband, Steven, were so happy to have the children living with them, the home was really the parent's domain since they were the ones paying the mortgage, bills, and other expenses. The bedrooms were the kid's domain. Jacqueline and Steven didn't have as high a tolerance for clutter as the kids did. They set up the system so that if the kids left their things in the parents' domain, it was at risk. In other words, if the kids left something out, Jacqueline might pick it up for them. If that happened, it might go straight to the Goodwill facility, never to be seen in their home again.

Jacqueline is not interested in picking up after her children. They know the consequences if she has to pick up after them. When Jacqueline sees something out of place during the day, she asks the child that left it out if they would like to pick it up or if they would like her to do it. The child always quickly jumps up and puts the item away.

It's now the children that face the consequences if they leave things out, not the parents. I asked Jacqueline if she really donated everything to the Goodwill facility. She said following through on her threat is absolutely vital. She has donated an entire Playstation system, high school textbooks, winter coats etc. Her children know she means business. *They* have to pay for the consequences of those things disappearing. Not her. Her attitude is if they left those things lying around at the school playground, they would never see them again. They can be just as careful not to leave things lying around in her domain. They caught on quickly.

This may seem a little extreme. But think about how much less nagging, arguing, and scolding would take place in the home if you followed Jacqueline's example. Think how less often your children would leave things behind at the school, at friend's houses, at the park. Think how much more clutter-free your home would be. I think it's a good idea. You just have to have the courage to really follow through on donating what you find to the Goodwill facility. Otherwise the whole system crashes.

Warning!

In working with your spouse and children you need to avoid upward delegation. Your children usually complain as a cleverly disguised attempt to get you to do the job.

If it's not a safety hazard, when they are complaining, offer a few words of encouragement and then leave the room. Phrases such as, "You're doing fine" and "You'll figure it out" will save you lots of headaches.

12

Conclusion

I n conclusion, let me review the Seven Steps of the organizing process and the Seven Strategies that cause your things to stay organized. To help you remember the steps and the order they come in, I have assigned them to the acronym of "E.N.D. C.H.A.O.S.".

E xamine Your Situation

aNd

D esign a Plan that Works for Your Unique Situation

C ategorize Your Things

H aul Them to Their New Destinations

A ssign the Right Home

O btain the Right Container

S ustain Your Systems Daily

Remember, there are Seven Steps in the organizing process. There are only Seven Steps and there are always Seven Steps. It is important you do the steps in the right order and it's important you complete each step before moving onto the next step. It is equally important you do **all** Seven Steps.

There are Seven Strategies that cause your things to *stay* organized. My motto is "Minimum Maintenance" so you can spend your time pursuing higher goals or enjoying your hobbies. Break free of clutter and chaos. At the same time, break free of hours and hours of maintenance.

The Seven Strategies are:

1) Do all Seven Steps of the organizing process.

2) Maintain a proper fit between your things and the containers you are putting them in, and between your containers and the space you are putting the containers in.

3) Store everything at the place where it is first used. Inside its region so it's within arms' reach.

4) Make it easier to put things away than it is to get them out.

5) Eliminate extra steps in the putting away process.

6) Label everything.

7) Maintain it daily.

If you follow the Seven Steps and Seven Strategies, you'll save yourself two hours a day.

Not only will you save yourself from hours of clutter control, but you'll function so much more efficiently, you'll be able to get all your tasks done in a fraction of the time it is currently taking you.

Where to Begin?

So where do you begin? How do you take all this information and apply it in a manner that makes sense? I'll get you started. I'll give you the first 20 steps to get the ball rolling.

Step #1 Decide on the pace you want to set for transforming your home. One region a week, or one room a week, or one room a month. Don't stress out. Make the transformation at a pace you can comfortably keep up with.

Step #2 Map out your master plan. Sketch out your floor plan. Make a list of the regions you want to have in your home (see the regions I listed in Chapter 9). Number the regions and write the numbers on your floor plan sketch.

Step #3 Choose which region you want to start with. I recommend you start with a very small region such as the Entry region (closet). After you have completed your first region successfully it will fuel your energies to do additional regions.

Step #4 Now go to Chapter 3. Examine your situation as it pertains to the region you have decided to work on. Carefully consider each part of the examination. Write down your conclusions.

Step #5 Go to Chapter 4. Apply everything that pertains to the region you are working on. Design solutions for all the habits, style, priorities, and needs you discovered during your examination.

Step #6 Take your ideas and run them past the Seven Strategies checklist. Brainstorm on how you can implement the Seven Strategies even better. Open your mind to all possibilities.

Step #7 Make your table of what supplies would belong in the region, and what containers will be right for the supplies you will be storing.

Step #8 Decide your parameters of how much space you are going to dedicate to that region. When you de-clutter you have to consider that pre-determined amount of space and get rid of items until you fit within your chosen parameters.

Step #9 Speed-sort! Get everything out of that regions space that has nothing to do with that regions activity.

Step #10 Gather all supplies for that region and bring them together to the regions location. Go to all corners of the house and get all supplies pertaining to the region you are working on.

Step #11 Speed-sort through the supplies you have gathered. Insist on creating a proper fit within your regions space.

Step #12 Go to Chapter 6. Follow the guidelines on how to assign the right homes for the items that belong inside this region.

Step #13 Go to Chapter 7. Follow the guidelines on how to find the right containers. Insist on a proper fit. Eliminate extra motions. Make the putting away process as easy as possible.

Step #14 Purchase the containers needed for the region you are working on. Install contents into the containers. Label the container and the space the container belongs.

Step #15 Begin today to do the "10-Minute Sweep" on the region you have finished.

Step #16 Choose a second region to work on. It should be in the same room as the first region you did. Follow steps 4-15 with your second region. Refer to Chapter 9 for suggestions on how to set up certain regions.

Step #17 Watch for items being left out in the regions you have transformed. Ask yourself which of the Seven Strategies has not been implemented as much as it could have been. Make refinements. Expect that you'll need to improve your implementation of the Seven Strategies after you've completed the region. Make refinements until clean up is a snap.

Step #18 Now choose the third region you want to work on. You should complete all the regions in a room before working on regions in different rooms. That makes it easy to do the "10-Minute Sweep" and decide what space is included in the sweep.

Step #19 Do steps 4 – 15 and step 17 with the third region. Continue this process until you have transformed the entire house.

Step #20 Notice how much of the house is clutter-free after the "10-Minute Sweep" is done for the day. Rejoice in your new found freedom. Make plans of what you want to do with all your spare time.

Reduce clutter, free your time and energy by minimizing maintenance. Create an environment of love, harmony, and positive energy. Be able to find anything in your home within just a few seconds. Improve your image and quality of life. It's time to enjoy your home again!

My mission is to influence the lives of thousands of people to the better by teaching them organizing skills for the home and workplace. I hope you will accept my challenge to read this book several times, attend my presentations several times and work day-by-day to transform your home and your life. I hope you will spread my word to others. Don't share my book or copy it. It is my life's work. Help your friends get their own copy so they can digest these principles morsel after morsel. So they can enjoy all the benefits mentioned in these final paragraphs.

Thank you for taking the time to study these principles.

Minimize the maintenance. Break free!!

About the author

Christi Youd is one of the most outstanding professional organizers in the organizing industry. She has been quoted and featured in numerous newspapers and magazines, and on popular radio and television programs.

She is the President of Organize Enterprise LLC; a Utah-based professional organizing company. Serving and satisfying client after client, she has built a solid reputation as an energetic, intelligent, problem-solving organizer who designs and implements systems that last.

Christi helps companies improve their bottom line by doing more in less time. Her research shows that she has boosted many of their levels of productivity by as much as 25%. She is a consultant for businesses and associations in organizing workspace and managing tasks and time. She helps individuals get ahead in the professional world by improving their image, increasing their productivity, and reducing their stress level.

She helps people conquer the clutter in their homes and sets up systems so their homes will stay organized. Her methods have helped thousands of people to get a grip on their hectic lives.

Trained by the National Association of Professional Organizers, and having twenty years of experience in the business world, Christi has mastered the principles and practices of organization, time management, and paper management. She uses her knowledge and skills to help people move from chaos to order in their home and workplace. She is past-president of the Utah Association of Professional Organizers (UTAPO).

Christi is a member of the National Speakers Association. She speaks on different facets of organizing your life. Speaking is Christi's favorite part of her business, because she can teach so many people how to organize for themselves and she can make a difference that lasts a lifetime.

As a speaker and presenter, Christi is known for her funny

stories, great ideas, professional manner, and friendly attitude. She has been speaking, writing, and conducting training programs for over 15 years. Her background in sales, business, and home management has contributed to the foundation for her work as an organizer and speaker.

Christi's newsletter <u>An Organized Life</u> has appeared monthly throughout the country. Her articles on getting organized have been published throughout the state of Utah and on the Internet. To subscribe to her free newsletter submit your email address to *christi@OrganizeEnterprise.com*.

Her best selling book "Organize Your Home in 10 Minutes a Day" (formerly titled "Minimize the Maintenance") is changing lives and has been selected by her clients as required reading for family and friends. She is also the author of "Organize Your Office for Success."

Christi Youd is available for consultations, organizing services, interviews, professional speaking engagements, and workshops.

Send request via email to:
christi@OrganizeEnterprise.com
or by calling (801) 756-3382

Need More In-Depth Help to Thoroughly De-Clutter Your Home?

Get Christi Youd's "30 Days to a Clutter-Free Home" Coaching Program!

Clutter can really take a toll on your sanity – let Christi show you how to do it correctly…step-by-step.

If clutter in your home is holding you and your family back from achieving the happiness and unity that you want to feel, then this program is designed to help YOU.

Christi will guide you every step of the way to clear out the clutter from every room in your home – GUARANTEED!

And as the clutter disappears, so will your feelings of anger, defeat, and being overwhelmed. This coaching program really works!

By tapping into Christi's expertise and experience through this coaching program, you'll actually be getting more of her for the money than if you hired her to do the work for you. It's the best win-win opportunity to clear out the clutter from your home once and for all!

For complete details about the "30 Days to a Clutter-Free Home" Coaching Program, see the back of this book for contact information.

Great News!
"Organize Your Home" is Now Available as an Audio Book on CD!

This is your chance to truly master all of the priceless tips, tricks, and techniques in this book while <u>driving</u>, <u>exercising</u>, or <u>just listening</u>!

- Perfect if you have no time to read...

- ...or find the printed version difficult to focus on...

- ...or you want to turn your daily drive into an "Organizing University"...

- ...need another way to master these valuable principles!

Now you can use your spare time to truly MASTER these life-changing organizing principles!

This book on audio CD will quickly become a very important part of your life because it allows you to learn by listening, which will enhance the learning you've gained from reading the book. You'll get all the same great information, including the specific STEP-BY-STEP BLUEPRINT of what you need to do to transform your home into the environment you dream of, but in convenient audio CD format!

You'll discover that *Organize Your Home* is NOT just a bunch of vague ideas like you'll find in other books. I've developed a system that you can use to maintain with literally just a few minutes of effort each day. <u>That's exactly</u> why it works. Because I focused on helping you in the REAL WORLD, not some make-believe magazine lifestyle.

To order your copy of the "Organize Your Home" audio book on CD, see the back of this book for details on how to contact us.

Hire Christi to Speak at Your Next Event!

Christi Youd has achieved recognition of one of the outstanding professional organizers in the industry. She has been quoted and featured in numerous newspapers and magazines and on popular radio and television programs.

As a speaker and presenter, Christi is known for her funny stories, great ideas, professional manner, and friendly attitude. She has been speaking, writing, and conducting training programs for over 15 years. Her background in sales, business, and home management has contributed to the foundation for her work as an organizer and speaker. Whether you need a keynote, half day, or full day training program Christi can deliver for you.

Christi speaks on Residential Organizing...

Professional Organizer, Christi Youd, teaches organizing skills that will help you organize your home and everything in it. Her seven strategies cause your things to STAY organized. Break free of clutter and chaos. At the same time, break free of hours of maintenance. You'll see demonstrations on how to organize your paperwork, clothing, toys, games, and more. You'll cut your time dealing with these things by 50%.

Christi speaks on Corporate Organizing

To help your staff be more efficient, productive, and professional, you'll want to schedule Organize Enterprise's in-house training workshop. It's a four hour workshop that teaches your staff how to organize their own space to be more efficient and productive. They'll learn to process documents, communications, tasks, ideas, and anything else necessary to get their work done. In addition, they'll learn to master the skills of prioritizing, discarding, delegating, streamlining their work, handling interruptions, avoiding procrastination, prompt filing, and much more. This training is guaranteed to improve the way your company does business.

Christi speaks on the Psychology of Change

It's not enough to know how to organize. We need to know how to get ourselves to DO what we KNOW. In order to create lasting change in our environment we must first make some changes in our psyche. Christi teaches easy step by step instructions that can help anyone take control of their mindset and attitude about organizing. You'll be amazed at how easy and consistent lasting change can be.

Contact Christi Youd at
Christi@OrganizeEnterprise.com – or – 801-756-3382

Printed in the United States
98949LV00004B/243/A

9 780615 151274